ASP.NET 3.5
Application Architecture and Design

Build robust, scalable ASP.NET applications quickly
and easily

Vivek Thakur

PUBLISHING

BIRMINGHAM - MUMBAI

ASP.NET 3.5

Application Architecture and Design

First published: October 2008

Production Reference: 1171008

Published by Packt Publishing Ltd.
32 Lincoln Road
Olton
Birmingham, B27 6PA, UK.

ISBN 978-1-847195-50-0

www.packtpub.com

Cover Image by Nilesh Mohite (nilpreet2000@yahoo.co.in)

Credits

Author

Vivek Thakur

Reviewers

Jerry Spohn

Ian Robinson

Tim Eisenhauer

Acquisition Editor

Adil Rizwan Ahmed

Development Editor

Ved Prakash Jha

Technical Editors

Rakesh Shejwal

Shadab Khan

Editorial Team Leader

Akshara Aware

Project Manager

Abhijeet Deobhakta

Project Coordinator

Lata Basantani

Indexer

Monica Ajmera

Proofreader

Dirk Manuel

Copy Editor

Sumathi Sridhar

Production Coordinator

Shantanu Zagade

Cover Work

Shantanu Zagade

About the Author

Vivek Thakur is passionate about architecting and developing applications based on the Microsoft .NET platform using ASP.NET, C#, VB.NET, and MS AJAX. He has authored several technical articles on ASP.NET and has also been an All-Star-level contributor on the ASP.NET forums. Vivek's passion for ASP.NET has been formally recognized by way of the Most Valuable Professional (MVP) award given to him by Microsoft in April 2007, and again in 2008. He is also a Subject Matter Expert for Microsoft ASP.NET 3.5 Certification Exams. He is a leading contributor and moderator in the CodeAsp.Net forums. Vivek is currently working as the Managing Partner in Axero Solutions LLC, a US-based software product development and business consulting firm.

Although his expertise lies in Microsoft's .NET platform, Vivek is also knowledgeable on J2EE and C/C++. He has a deep interest in programming, chaos theory, and artificial intelligence, and is a strong advocate of chaos theory in software systems and management.

Besides his love for software architecture and design, Vivek also focuses on project management skills and has substantial experience in managing small to medium sized projects. He has also conducted numerous training sessions and provided concept-based tutoring for different software firms across India.

Vivek received his Bachelors degree in engineering from the Indian Institute of Technology (IIT), New Delhi, India.

Writing this book would not have been possible without the support of my family and friends. My sincere gratitude to my mother Sharda Thakur, father G.C Thakur, and my sisters Isha and Shikha Thakur for their continued support and encouragement while I was writing this book. Special thanks to my friend Kritika Srinivasan for her incessant support throughout.

I would like to acknowledge Tim Eisenhauer for his extended support while technically reviewing the book, and also for his extended efforts in discussing and providing feedback on many topics.

I would like to thank Ian Robinson and Jerry Spohn for their relentless efforts in technical reviews and making sure that I do not miss out on core technical issues. Thanks to Ved for his detailed feedback and help in solving basic queries.

Also, many thanks to our technical editors Rakesh and Shadab, and our Production Coordinator Shantanu.

About the Reviewers

Ian Robinson is a Software Developer at Engage Software. Originally from Southern Illinois, Ian moved to the St. Louis, Missouri area in 2001 to attend Webster University. After a stint as an intern at a large St. Louis based corporation, Ian graduated with a degree in Computer Science and subsequently joined the team at Engage Software, where he enjoys developing web-based solutions for clients, as well as developing commercial modules for DotNetNuke. Focusing primarily on development within the DotNetNuke web application framework, Ian has notably developed enterprise-level solutions for businesses in the healthcare and mobile industries. He is also a lead instructor for Engage Software's Official DotNetNuke Training, training businesses and individuals on DotNetNuke administration and development in St. Louis and throughout the United States. Ian Robinson is currently working and living in St. Louis Missouri with his wife Lucy.

Jerry Spohn is a Manager of Development for a medium-sized software development firm in Exton, Pennsylvania. His responsibilities include managing a team of developers and assisting in architecting a large, multi-lingual, multi-currency loan account system, written in COBOL and JAVA. He is also responsible for maintaining and tracking a system-wide program and database documentation web site, for which he uses DotNetNuke as the portal for this information.

Jerry is also the owner of Spohn Software LLC., a small consulting firm that helps small businesses in the area of maintaining and improving their business processes. This includes helping with the creation and maintenance of web sites, general office productivity issues, and computer purchasing and networking. Spohn Software, as a firm, prefers to teach their clients how to solve their problems internally, rather than require a long-term contract, thereby making the business more productive and profitable in the future.

Jerry currently works and resides in Pennsylvania, with his wife, Jacqueline, and his two sons, Nicholas and Nolan.

Tim Eisenhauer has 11+ years of website architecture and development experience with a focus on usability design, user interface, and web engineering. Tim is skilled in creating state-of-the-art GUI designs for the ASP.NET platform, built for SEO optimization design, along with a pure-CSS design structure. Tim also has practical hands-on experience in developing content management systems, CRM, ERP, innovative web design ideas and SEO friendly web applications. He also specializes in branding and marketing consulting to help Web 2.0+ businesses succeed and strengthen their position in the extremely competitive e-commerce, B2B, and B2C markets.

Tim has strong exposure to linking creativity and usability with ever changing modern day business scenarios. Strong visual branding and sharp reasoning skills coupled with in-depth technical know-how places Tim amongst a rare breed of technical leaders who can not only help shape businesses up from ground-zero but also help them stand distinctly apart from the crowd.

I dedicate this book to
my grandparents Sh. Roop Chand Thakur and Smt. Nirmala Devi.

Table of Contents

Preface

The world of web development, as we see today, has undergone many dynamic changes shaped by multiple new technologies and platforms. Over the last few years Microsoft ASP.NET has quickly evolved to become one of the most famous platforms for developing web-based solutions. Since early 2002, when the first version (1.0) of ASP.NET was released, Microsoft has continuously added many out-of-the-box features and components, making web development easier for the end developer. In a very short time span, the ASP.NET platform has grown and matured into a stable object-oriented framework, with a large set of useful tools and a huge class library, attracting widespread interest in the developer communities around the world. With the introduction of LINQ, MS AJAX, WCF, WPF, and a lot of exciting new tools, the .NET framework has not only grown large but also flexible, in terms of the choices and options being offered to the developers.

With all of these new technologies hogging the limelight, an ever-increasing gap was created in the mindset of new developers, due to a shift in priorities. Developers, especially beginners, were attracted by the buzz created by these new, cool tools, and started interpreting them as a solution for better architecture and design, losing focus on the core concepts in the process. A developer, who has just learnt the basics of ASP.NET, was more eager to devote his or her time to technologies such as AJAX and LINQ instead of learning and implementing design patterns.

One reason for this paradigm shift was the lack of books that could showcase a better way to structure and develop ASP.NET-based web solutions, explaining with examples how to use different architectural styles and design patterns in real-life ASP.NET code. This book aims to bridge that gap.

I won't be focusing on deep and detailed theoretical concepts, as this book is not a "pure" architecture and design guide. Rather, the goal is to show you how to design a web site in ASP.NET the correct way, focus on different design options, analyze and study what architectural options we have, and decide when to use which architectural solution. It is very important to understand that there is no one perfect or best way in architecture and design. We need to improvise, and adapt to each project's unique requirements. Understanding core application architecture and design patterns can be tough for many developers, and so this book aims to elucidate these through the use of real-life examples and code in ASP.NET. This book will also shed some light on the basics of better application structure, coding practices, and database design, and will demonstrate, with suitable examples, how the correct architectural decisions can greatly impact overall application stability and performance.

What This Book Covers

Chapter 1 will introduce you to architecture and design in ASP.NET, including tiers, layers, and logical structuring.

Chapter 2 discusses the advantages and disadvantages of using the simplest and easiest 1-tier, 1-layer default architecture in ASP.NET. You will also understand when and why we should use out-of-the-box data source controls, and how the 1-tier, 1-layer style is tightly-coupled and is not flexible or scalable.

Chapter 3 discusses what an ER diagram is, the domain model, the basics of UML, and what an n-layer design is, and how it increases the flexibility and maintainability of the code when compared to a 1-layer architecture. A sample project is explained with code in a 3-layer model. The drawbacks or limitations of this model are also discussed.

Chapter 4 talks about n-tier architecture in ASP.NET and how to implement it. It also explains Data Transfer Objects and how to use them with 4-tier and 5-tier web solutions.

In *Chapter 5*, you will learn and understand what MVC design is, and how the ASP.NET MVC framework helps us quickly implement MVC design in our web applications.

In *Chapter 6*, you will learn how and when to use the most common design patterns in ASP.NET: Factory, Dependency Injection, Singleton, and others.

Chapter 7 explains why we need SOA, explaining the advantages of SOA for a beginner. A sample project using SOA architecture is discussed. The chapter also explains how the Windows Communication Framework (WCF) compliments SOA.

Chapter 8 deals with the importance of a well-designed database, balanced normalization, logical and physical models, and tips and tricks for better database models.

Chapter 9 covers localization for ASP.NET applications, the deployment of localized applications, the localization framework, and best practices.

What You Need for This Book

Readers should be familiar with and know how to use:

- Visual Studio 2008.
- SQL Server 2005.
- Operating system: Code samples will run both on Windows XP Pro and Windows Vista, Windows 2003/2008.
- Microsoft Visio Enterprise Architect (you can use the trial version available free to download from MS website). This is needed only for one of the chapters (Chapter 8).

Who is This Book For

Readers must have basic understanding of the ASP.NET framework, and programming knowledge of either C# or VB.NET. The book can be used by any ASP.NET developer. Although it is primarily aimed at beginner and intermediate developers, it is a good resource for experienced programmers as well. This book is not a theoretical guide on architecture and design patterns, or any other technology.

If reading about application architecture usually confuses you or sends you to sleep, then this book will be perfect for you! In short, any ASP.NET programmer who is confused or disoriented after reading different books or materials on architectures, or is wondering how and what to implement in their application, will definitely benefit from this book!

Conventions

In this book, you will find a number of styles of text that distinguish between different kinds of information. Here are some examples of these styles, and an explanation of their meaning.

Code words in text are shown as follows: "We are just calling the `GetAllProducts()` method, which has all data access code wrapped in a different class named DAL."

A block of code will be set as follows:

```
<asp:Repeater ID="prodRepeater" runat="server">
    <ItemTemplate>
        Product Code:  <%# Eval("Code")%>
            <br>
        Name:          <%# Eval("Name")%>
            <br>
        Unit Price:  $<%# Eval("UnitPrice")%>
            <br>
    </ItemTemplate>
</asp:Repeater>
```

New terms and **important words** are introduced in a bold-type font. Words that you see on the screen, in menus or dialog boxes for example, appear in our text like this: "In the Internet Explorer, we can change the default language by going to **Internet Options** and clicking the **Language** button under the **General** tab."

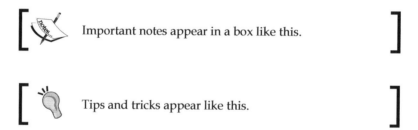

Important notes appear in a box like this.

Tips and tricks appear like this.

Reader Feedback

Feedback from our readers is always welcome. Let us know what you think about this book, what you liked or may have disliked. Reader feedback is important for us to develop titles that you really get the most out of.

To send us general feedback, simply drop an email to feedback@packtpub.com, making sure to mention the book title in the subject of your message.

If there is a book that you need and would like to see us publish, please send us a note in the **SUGGEST A TITLE** form on www.packtpub.com or email suggest@packtpub.com.

If there is a topic that you have expertise in and you are interested in either writing or contributing to a book, see our author guide on www.packtpub.com/authors.

Customer Support

Now that you are the proud owner of a Packt book, we have a number of things to help you to get the most from your purchase.

Downloading the Example Code for the Book

Visit http://www.packtpub.com/files/code/5500_Code.zip to directly download the example code.

Errata

Although we have taken every care to ensure the accuracy of our contents, mistakes do happen. If you find a mistake in one of our books—maybe a mistake in text or code—we would be grateful if you would report this to us. By doing this you can save other readers from frustration, and help to improve subsequent versions of this book. If you find any errata, report them by visiting http://www.packtpub.com/support, selecting your book, clicking on the **let us know** link, and entering the details of your errata. Once your errata are verified, your submission will be accepted and the errata added to the list of existing errata. The existing errata can be viewed by selecting your title from http://www.packtpub.com/support.

Piracy

Piracy of copyright material on the Internet is an ongoing problem across all media. At Packt, we take the protection of our copyright and licenses very seriously. If you come across any illegal copies of our works in any form on the Internet, please provide the location address or website name immediately so we can pursue a remedy.

Please contact us at copyright@packtpub.com with a link to the suspected pirated material.

We appreciate your help in protecting our authors, and our ability to bring you valuable content.

Questions

You can contact us at questions@packtpub.com if you are having a problem with some aspect of the book, and we will do our best to address it.

1

Introduction to Architecture and Design

Almost every software developer I know is fascinated by software architecture and design. High-level architecture and design patterns are concepts that beginner developers least understand. For most of us, programming is relatively easier to learn; usually good aptitude and decent logical skills are enough to be a good programmer. But architecture is altogether a different beast to handle. It is more of an art, and usually takes years of experience to master.

In this chapter, we will focus on:

- Understanding architecture and design from a practical viewpoint
- Architectural styles
- What Design patterns are
- Different stages of a project lifecycle
- Difference between tiers and layers

Software Architecture

There are many different definitions of software architecture scattered across the web, in reference materials, and in books. In the wide world of programming, many of the definitions you may find are most likely going to be extremely technical in the language they use, and can be difficult for a beginner to fully grasp and understand. There are even places on the web that list thousands and thousands of different definitions by leading software architects, engineers, doctors, philosophers, and professors. (Reference: `http://www.sei.cmu.edu/architecture/community_definitions.html`).

To begin with, let's start with a technical definition:

> *Software architecture is an abstraction, or a high-level view of the system. It focuses on aspects of the system that are most helpful in accomplishing major goals, such as reliability, scalability, and changeability. The architecture explains how you go about accomplishing those goals.*

Now we will translate this definition into something simple, generic, and easy to understand:

```
Software architecture is a blueprint of your application.
```

To elaborate more on the "blueprint" part, let us try to understand software architecture with a simple analogy—the process of casting.

Casting is a manufacturing process in which a liquid material is poured into a mold that contains a hollow cavity of a desired shape. The liquid is then allowed to cool and solidify, taking the shape of the mold it was poured into. The mold is the guide that shapes the liquid into the intended result. Keep in mind that the mold can be of any shape, size, or dimension, and is separate or unrelated to the liquid that is poured in.

Now, think of software architecture as the mold and think of your project as the liquid that is poured into this mold. Just like casting, software architecture is the guide that shapes your project into the intended result. The architecture of a software system has no strict relation to the actual code that is written for this system. The architecture simply makes sure that the development process stays within certain defined limits.

Software Design

Software design refers to the thought process involved in planning and providing for a better solution during problem solving. Software design comes after the architecture is decided upon. Architecture is more closely related to the business needs of the project, and theoretically it does not concern the actual technology platform (such as J2EE or Microsoft .NET or PHP) on which the application will be built (although practically we can decide the platform either in parallel with working on the architecture of the application or before doing so). Software design deals with the high-level concepts related to the actual implementation of the architecture in our projects, which include tasks such as usability studies to make sure our project targets the right kind of users, deciding which design patterns to use to make our application scalable, secure and robust. During the design phase, we also decide on the implementation methodology to be used in the actual development phase (which comes after design and involves actual coding). The following diagram shows how architecture and design fit together and relate to each other:

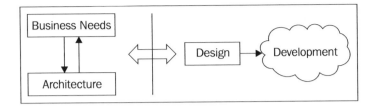

As we can see in the diagram, the actual business requirements and scope of the project are the deciding factors when working on the application architecture. Software design and development come next and, based on the design, the actual development work gets executed. A single problem can have many possible solutions, some of which will be more efficient than others. Before a developer starts chunking out code for a particular business requirement, it would be prudent and beneficial to give some thought and select the best approach from the possible list of options to assure that code performance, scalability and maintainability is not sacrificed in the long run.

In order to understand all of this by way of a simple analogy, consider a car manufacturing plant as an example. The mechanical engineers developing the high-level blueprint of the car would be the architects, and the blueprint itself would be the architecture of the car. This blueprint would include high-level specifications such as:

- Dimensions of the car and its components
- Engine capacity
- Type of car (hatchback, sedan, or SUV)
- Maximum passenger capacity, and load capacity
- Minimum build strength

So the blueprint would specify the limitations as well as the conditions that need to be fulfilled for any design of that car, and besides the blueprint there would be additional constraints such as the budget for the production costs. But this blueprint would not include details of how exactly the engine would be designed, what quality of steel would be used, what type of tires would be used, what type of plastics would be used for the dashboard and other parts, and so on. All of this would actually be decided by the design engineers, who will make sure that their choices fit the blueprint specifications in the best possible way. The engineers will also consider production and design techniques that other car companies might have followed, so that they don't re-invent the wheel.

The actual assembly line production will follow the designs and techniques specified by the engineers and will involve tasks such as cutting metal, choosing the right machines, assembling the individual components, painting, safety tests, and so on, to create a complete working car. The following figure will correlate this example with the equivalent aspects of software development:

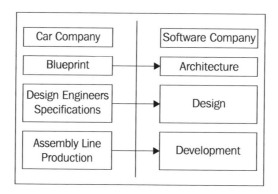

From the figure we can see how the car company example loosely translates to software architecture, design, and development. Now let us take another analogy, this time more closely related to the software industry. Consider a company that needs to build a bulk emailing program for its social networking website. A software architect will first understand the high-level requirements of the program, such as:

- How many average emails need to be sent on a daily or hourly basis?
- How often will the emails need to be sent?
- Will there be attachments involved? If yes, what will be the biggest attachment size?
- Does this program need to be extensible and re-usable (for other similar websites or applications in that company)?

Based on the answers to the above questions, the architect will come up with an application architecture which covers all aspects of the actual business needs. The architecture will decide how the emailing program should be developed: a Windows Service, or a Web Service, or a console utility, or some batch program run by a scheduler.

But the architecture would not include details such as:

- How should the program handle exceptions?
- How will we make sure that the code is efficient in terms of performance, and does not hang while sending bulk emails in a short period?

- How should the program perform error logging?
- How will the program be developed so that it is re-usable (if the architecture dictates it to be developed as a re-usable component)?

That's the part where design comes into the picture. The application architecture would define limits and boundaries within which the design would move around and improvise. So the architecture would neither go deep into the nitty-gritties of the design phase, nor would it dictate implementation guidelines and programming rules, as the architecture has no relation with programming at all. In fact, the architecture lays out specifications which are more aligned with business requirements, and makes sure that all business aspects are met and taken care of.

Coming back to our bulk email program, the term software design can be loosely translated into the process of designing the actual program, which involves using specific programming techniques (or design patterns, which we will study later) and laying out the basic solution framework. All coding would actually occur within that framework. We can have multiple design options for the same architectural specification, and it is up to the stakeholders to decide which one to go for, considering the overall efficiency and budget constraints.

Here is a simple diagram illustrating the basic process:

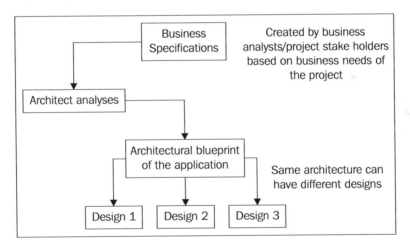

Architectural Styles

With time, some of the famous and widely used approaches and techniques among the architects have been grouped together into architectural styles. A particular architectural style represents the interaction and behavior pattern between the system and its components, along with a particular layout and structure. Some famous architectural styles are:

- n-tier model
- Windows DNA
- Data-centric
- Service Oriented Architecture
- Plug-in system

There are many more styles, and each style can be customized to suit individual project needs. We will learn more about some of these styles in the coming chapters, along with some practical examples. It is very important to understand the concept, approach, and effective implementation of a style so that we can decide when to use which style in our own applications. One can even create a new style by combining any of the existing styles and customizing it to achieve greater efficiency and adaptability.

Architecture and Design in ASP.NET

But, as we look to the horizon of a decade hence, we see no silver bullet. There is no single development, in either technology or in management technique that by itself promises even one order-of-magnitude improvement in productivity, in reliability, in simplicity.

The above quote (taken from *No Silver Bullet – essence and accident in software Engineering*, Brooks, F. P.) aptly highlights the fact that technological improvements can only be stepping stones instead of being silver bullets to solve all architectural and design problems in one go. The ASP.NET platform has rapidly gained a foothold in the web development industry. One of the major factors in favor of ASP.NET, compared to JAVA or PHP, is the excellent integration of the Microsoft IDE, Visual Studio, with the framework. The VS IDE has evolved, complementing the framework itself, with time-saving features such as detailed intelligence support, debugging assistant, and code complete, to list a few. Also, Microsoft has been aggressively adding different tools and technologies, enhancing the overall developer experience. AJAX, LINQ, WCF, WWF and SilverLight have not only stirred up the development world but have also left many developers confused and wondering as to how good these new technologies are, and how they can maximize their productivity by using them.

Some developers strongly feel that these new technologies are coming along much faster than they can be absorbed. There have been many heated debates on the extra aggressiveness with which Microsoft is releasing new products. In many of the offline discussions we have had upto now, most people feel that developers are not getting enough time to absorb existing technologies and "keep pace with MS". People are still struggling with master pages and partial classes, and we have AJAX, SilverLight, WPF, etc.!

Many developers feel that there is simply too much to grasp in too little time, considering the fact that many clients are still using VS2003 and are refusing to upgrade due to reasons such as lack of funds, apprehension of going with new and untested technologies such as WPF and Silverlight, lack of experienced programmers, and so on. Some customers are also confused and are not sure how these new technologies can benefit their business!

We should understand that none of the new technologies were created to be "silver bullets". They have been added to give developers options to chose from, to reduce development time, and to be more effective. These technologies should be used in the right architectural context instead of blindly following them, which can lead to a greater risk through poor implementation. All changes are good, but we need to understand why the change is needed and how it will help us in balancing the advantages and disadvantages.

We have thousands of books, online articles and tutorials on how to use AJAX, LINQ, WWF, and WPF in ASP.NET, but there are still very few online articles and limited books that focus on what architecture to use, and in which ASP.NET application. Because each project is unique in its own way, we can never use a copy-paste solution. The important thing to bar in mind when learning application architecture and design is that there are no strict rules, only guidelines. And these guidelines were developed based on the experience gained over years of work by developers on different projects.

Upcoming latest technologies should not be mistaken as the means to develop better applications. Lets go back to the pre-ASP.NET years for a moment. In those days, classic ASP was very famous. There were many big, famous, and stable applications in classic ASP 3.0. It was difficult to create an object-oriented application with classic ASP (compared to the intuitive way, in which we can do it so easily now in ASP. NET), but good programmers used classes in ASP as well, adopting elements of object-oriented re-usable design. A better platform, such as ASP.NET, did help in building websites that could support a better architecture, but the power to use it in an efficient way still lies in the hands of an experienced programmer.

Just as ASP.NET was a major stepping stone in web development, AJAX enhanced the UI experience along the same lines, providing a user-friendly experience while browsing websites, and LINQ was introduced to revolutionize data access. But still there are numerous robust and popular websites in ASP.NET not using any of the new technologies. This means that the key to building a good website can never only be learning and absorbing the latest technology out there, but also how you put it to use—how you make these technologies work for your project in a comprehensive way.

If one knows how to write clean and maintainable code and use efficient programming techniques to create a good stable architectural platform and application structure, then technology will supplement the design. Without a stable architecture and good coding practices, a programmer might use the technologies in a haphazard manner, creating messy code and junk websites. But once we understand basics of the application architecture and the different design patterns, then these technology tools become our assets.

Technology and Art

Unlike coding, which demands strong logical skills, application architecture and design is more of an art, and it takes time and experience to become a good architect. For example, it takes a very good and experienced designer to create a unique and attractive design for a car. Once it's done, the assembly line can create millions of units of that model using the appropriate machines and tools for the job. Similarly, it is relatively easier to understand and code in ASP.NET, but it can take some time for even an intermediate developer to be able to understand and design the pros and cons of the different architectural options that might suit a given web application. And unlike coding, there are no strict rules in architecture. A design which might not work for some projects can work perfectly well for others. That's why it might take years of experience to develop an eye for good architecture and design. This, coupled with the fact that each application is unique in its own sense and warrants its own design and architecture, can be confusing for developers when deciding what is best for their project.

Therefore, architecture is one thing which requires patient understanding, as well as creativity in order to be able to adapt and innovate according to a project's needs.

Architecture: First Steps

How do business requirements dictate architectural decisions? Lets understand this through a quick and small example. Assume that a software company, Takshila Inc., has recently bagged the contract for building a new inventory management system for a local cosmetics manufacturing firm. After the initial talks with the stakeholders, the business analyst from Takshila comes up with high-level specifications, which are:

- The system should be accessible from any online location
- The system should be able to process multiple orders at the same time
- The system should be able to interact and process information from different locations having different databases
- The system should interact with other software packages (such as financial software) already in use by the company
- The system should be easy to customize later by the internal development team

With these requirements in mind, and after detailed discussions with team members, the software architect has come up with the following architectural specifications for the proposed inventory management software:

- The system should be web based, using a thin-client architecture.
- The system should have built-in multithreading capabilities.
- The system should be database-independent, which means that the system should be able to work with multiple types of databases without changing the code — probable use of dependency injection.
- The system should expose a set of functions as an API, and should also be able to import data from other sources and process this data in its own tables.
- The system should have loosely-coupled tiers, so that each individual tier has no dependency on the other and can be used with any other tier.

Note how the business requirements have been translated into architectural specifications, and still there is not a word about a programming or development platform! So the architecture has nothing to do with development platforms, programming languages, design and so on. We can create a system satisfying the above requirements in many ways, using different designs and probably using different platforms too (for example, one could either use ASP.NET or JSP/J2EE). In short, the architecture does not care whether you use LINQ, AJAX, or Ruby on Rails. As long as you are meeting the architectural specifications, you are free to choose your own technology and tools.

Design Patterns

The word *pattern* means a guide or a model that is to be followed when making things. In software development, we often use programming techniques and solutions developed by others that prove to be credible over time. Solutions to software problems were not developed overnight, and most of these problems were common across the development world, so these time-tested solutions were grouped to be re-used by others.

So a design pattern is a re-usable solution that can be used in our projects so that time-tested programming techniques can be employed to solve similar kinds of problems.

The main difference between architecture and design patterns is that design patterns deal with implementation-level issues, and are more close to the programming and development platform, whereas architecture is at a more abstract level and is independent of the implementation. Design patterns tell us how we can achieve a solution in terms of implementation. But the patterns themselves are independent of the programming language and technology platform. We can implement a particular design pattern in any language we want: JAVA, C# or PHP. We cannot use design patterns as-it-is in our projects. They show us the right path to take in order to solve a problem, but they are not a complete solution. We cannot simply copy-paste a particular design pattern's code directly into our project. We will need to modify it to suit our own unique needs and implementation platform.

In the coming chapters, we will learn some of the famous design and commonly used patterns, with sample code in ASP.NET.

Project Life Cycle

From an idea to a fully functional binary or DLL, a project passes through a varied range of activities and processes. The project life cycle refers to the different logical and physical stages that a project goes through from inception to completion. The life cycle starts with gathering the business requirements and ends when the final product is delivered after complete testing. The following are the major stages of a generic project life cycle:

1. Project Initiation
2. Planning and Prototyping
3. Project Construction
4. Project Transition and Release

These stages are more-or-less common through all projects. In this section, we will see some of the basic processes and understand the importance of each. Note that it is not necessary for each project to follow a standard life cycle strictly. Every project will have its own modified version of the life cycle, as well as its own duration for each stage.

Project Initiation

This is the part where the project idea is discussed with the stakeholders. Here, we discuss the feasibility of the project, and decide if it is really worth moving forward with the project at all. A few things which might be discussed are:

- Does the project's business model make sense?
- Is the project feasible given the current technological platforms?
- How big is the project going to be? Is it possible to complete the project within the business deadline?
- Do we have the required technical talent available in the market to complete the project on time?

In this phase, the business analyst or the stakeholder(s) will create a high-level requirements document. This document will list the aim of the project and its fundamental business logic in business terms. One can also create RFQ (Request For Quotation) or RFI (Request For Information) documents to be sent to other firms who might be willing to bid for the development of the project, or to the internal development team for further development time and cost estimates.

So in this first stage, the stakeholders discuss and decide on the business feasibility of the project and prepare a document that captures most of the requirements at a very high level.

Project Planning and Prototyping

In this phase, we elaborate on the project requirements by capturing all business requirements in specially formatted documents called *use cases*, and then prepare a prototype as well as a project plan for the next stages of the project life cycle. Once the project initiation and inception stage is over and the project owners have selected a development team, the second phase starts, in which the architect or the development team leads and the project manager will work out a plan and a development cycle. In this phase, most of the major pre-development activities take place. These activities are described in more detail below:

Project Plan

The project manager will need to create a plan that will lay out all of the major tasks in the project life cycle, along with the resources and time required. Without a plan it would be very difficult to track and manage the progress of different stages of a project. The project plan at this stage might not be able to cover the actual development phase, because this will depend on the completion of the following tasks.

Use Case Design

The architect/business analysts will first start this phase by creating use cases, which can be simple documents explaining the interaction between the application and the end user. A "use case" lists the interaction steps sequentially, along with other possible paths for a single interaction with the user. Each use case should capture a specific scenario from end-to-end. It should also list all pre-conditions as well as post-conditions for that scenario. Here is a sample use case:

UseCase 1.10 User Login	
Description:	Actor gains access to system.
Actors:	All roles.
Trigger:	Actor invokes the application.
Pre-Conditions:	Not applicable
Post-Conditions:	Actor is successfully logged in to system.
Basic Flow:	BF1: Log on to Client

1. The System displays the Login screen.
2. The Actor enters:
   a. Email ID
   b. Password
3. The System validates the email ID and password.
4. The use case ends when the Actor is logged into the system. The System displays a list of messages sorted in chronological order, with links to Compose, Delete and Aggregate messages. The actor can select any of the links.

UseCase 1.10 User Login

Alternate Flows:	**AF1: Forgot Password**

The use case starts when the actor has not logged in and clicks Forgot Password link.

1. The System displays the Forgot Password screen.
2. The Actor enters his email address.
3. The Actor clicks on Send Password.
4. The use case ends when the System sends the new password to the actor's email address.

AF2: Change Password

The use case starts when the My Account action is invoked. The actor is already logged in.

1. The System displays the My Account screen.
2. The Actor clicks on Change Password.
3. The Actor enters the current password and the new password.
4. The Actor clicks on Change Password.

The use case ends when the System saves the new password.

Exception Flows:	none
Special Requirements:	None

There are many ways of creating use cases; we can also create them diagrammatically. But to keep things simple, we can follow the above use case, which is easier to understand. After the major use cases are covered, we can move to the next step in this elaboration phase, which is, prototyping.

Prototyping

The **Graphical User Interface (GUI)** of any project is one of the most critical areas in terms of its overall presence and credibility. And many projects are delayed because of repeated changes in the GUI throughout the project life cycle, adding to the frustration of the programmers. For web projects, designing a working prototype in HTML before starting to work on any other activity can be very helpful, for project stakeholders as well as developers. A working prototype means that the different HTML pages would be linked to each other (based on the use cases we covered earlier), and can use dummy data to give a realistic impression of the actual project.

A GUI prototype is not only a part of the **Proof of Concept (POC)**, but also forms an important extension of the project requirements specifications, in a graphical sense. Properly-linked HTML pages with some dummy data showing the important business process flows can be an indispensable tool, aiding in the visual understanding of the project, as well as answering all kinds of technical and business-related questions. That is why it is highly recommended to develop a prototype before starting the actual coding for a project.

Class Model

The architect and the technical lead will create an object model of the system, highlighting all important entities and how they will interact. We will learn more about how to create an object model in the coming chapters of this book.

Database Model

A database model would be created based on the class model described above. This data model, along with the object model and use cases, will help provide the development team with clear instructions, and paths to the targets and objectives. It is very common for a data model to be created before a class model. It's also very common for these two steps to be completed at the same time, as they are very closely related.

Based on the use cases, the prototype and the object/data models, the project manager, along with the architect and the team lead, will develop a project plan for the construction phase, in which the coding takes place. This plan will highlight the milestones as well as list all of the important deliverables of that phase.

Project Construction: Programming and Development

When all of the primary documentation is complete, the actual development work starts. The technical team will study the use cases and the object and data models, and start planning the delivery cycles. Here, we can use one of the following famous development methodologies:

- SCRUM Development
- Waterfall Model
- Agile Development/Extreme Programming (XP)
- Iterative Development

You can find more information about each of these techniques online via the list of references I have provided. There is a lot of online as well as offline text available on these methodologies. I personally prefer SCRUM development, which is a Chaos Theory based approach. In SCRUM, we have *sprint*, which is an iteration with a certain number of days (for example, 30) at the end of which the development team covers a certain set of use cases and lets the stakeholders see and test the application. During the next iteration, they cover more features, which are prioritized accordingly. Each iteration passes through a full software development cycle: planning, requirements, design, coding, testing, and documentation. The goal is to have an available release (without bugs) at the end of each iteration.

A major goal to be achieved by using this process is to allow the client to take their new product to market before it is completed in its entirety. We are also minimizing risk by developing highly-focused components in a short period of time. This development process will continue throughout all phases, promoting the release of components to a beta phase in a live environment as the life cycles are completed. The following are the major benefits or principles of the SCRUM method:

- Keeping things simple by chunking (or batching)
- Customer satisfaction through rapid, continuous delivery of useful software they can get their hands on
- Working software is delivered frequently (taking weeks rather than months)
- Working software is the primary measure of progress
- Late changes or additions in requirements are welcome and can be added to iterations with ease
- Close, daily cooperation between clients and developers
- Continuous attention to technical excellence and good design
- Regular adaptation to changing circumstances

Because the stakeholders can see and review the current application at the end of each sprint, it gives them a valuable opportunity to change anything they don't like. Changes made at a later stage (such as when all use cases are covered) would take a longer time to absorb into the application, and can sometimes derail the project completely.

Project Transition and Release

At the end of the last iteration, the project will be in *alpha stage*, which means that all of the main use cases are implemented. The alpha build of the software is the build delivered to the software testers, usually internal to the organization/community developing the software. Usually, no end users see this phase. Alpha stage software is never completely bug free, but functionally covers all use cases.

Once the alpha testing is over, the project moves to the beta phase, which means that external users/end users (outside the company or organization that developed the software) can now start checking the system and using it.

A **beta version** is the first version released outside of the organization or community that developed the software, for the purpose of evaluation or real-world testing. Beta level software generally includes all of the features, but may also include known issues and bugs of a less serious variety. Once the beta phase is over and all major bugs have been fixed, the project is in an RTM (Release To Manufacture) stage, or in the Gold Edition.

The following is a summary table showing all of the important project phases:

Project Stages	Project Pitfalls
1. Initiation: Understanding project needs from a very high-level perspective and conducting a small feasibility study	A poor feasibility study can hinder or block project progress later on; it is very important to see what really can be achieved and what cannot, given the current technological offerings
2(a) Planning: Understand the project needs comprehensively, develop business use cases, detailed project plan, high-level architecture, class diagrams, data model, sequence diagrams, prototype	Detailed planning and project management is the key here; without a well laid out plan the project is doomed to fail. Wrong estimates or an improper choice of architecture can sound the death knell for the project's progress
2(b) Development: Work iteratively on selected use cases, QA process follows	Lack of unit tests, deviations in architecture, patching and short circuiting code to avoid missing deadlines
3. Transition: Beta testing, release docs, deployment instructions, bug fixing	Without proper usability and integration testing, success is not possible
4. Support: Provide support after the Gold/RTM release	Good support is very crucial

Tiers and Layers

There is a misunderstanding that tier and layers are two different names for the same entity. The concept of tier and layers came into being with the need for identifying and segregating different parts of an application into separate connected components. This separation can be at two levels:

- Physical Separation
- Logical Separation

Physical Separation

In a tier-based architecture, we separate code physically into different assemblies (or a set of assemblies). For example, we may have a single assembly for the web project, and another one for the class project having business code. If we want to deploy our application across multiple servers, spanning different geographical locations, then we need to use an n-tier architecture (which we will study in the coming chapters of this book).

Logical Separation

Separating into layers mean that we logically separate the code, but the entire application will be a part of a single physical assembly (or a set of assemblies depending on the compilation model). We may put the code files into separate folders, each having its own namespace for easier code management and readability, but we won't have a separate assembly for each different namespace or part of the code. Also, unlike physical separation, it will not be possible to deploy parts of the application in a distributed manner.

So a "tier" is a unit of deployment, while a "layer" is a logical separation of responsibility within the code. A layer becomes a tier if it can be physically separated from the layers consuming it. Alternatively, a tier is a layer which could be physically separated from the layers consuming it.

 If we are using the Visual Studio 2005 Website model, then we may have a set of assemblies for each page/folder, whereas if we use a Web Application Project (WAP) model (similar to the one used in VS 2003) we will have only a single assembly for the entire project.

Let's say we have a simple online guestbook system, which is a web-based application developed in ASP.NET. Here is a simple flowchart in a very basic form:

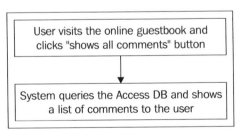

The user logs on to the website and visits the online guestbook, and clicks on the **show all comments** button. As a result, the system will show a list of comments to the user. For the same, the system sends a query to the Access DB, which in turn replies with a list of all the comments.

Now, one way to program this system is to create a simple web form with button, with the code to get the comments from the database placed inside the ASPX form (without using any code behind classes). The solution will compile into a single DLL. This inline coding approach will be discussed in the next chapter. Another method is to use code behind classes segregating the ASPX code and the C#/VB.NET code. We can introduce further loose coupling by separating the business logic and data access code into separate class library projects.

For a Windows-based project, also known as a **thick-client**, an n-tier project would have:

- Windows forms (or Windows Presentation Foundations, WPF) as the Presentation layer
- C# or VB.NET code handling the business logic as the Business Layer (BL)
- Data access code as the Data Access Layer (DAL)
- The physical database as the Data Layer (DL)

Data access layer (DAL) is a set of classes used to encapsulate data access methods like CRUD (Create Read Update and Delete) operations as well as any other methods accessing data from a data store (known as Data Layer). DAL's primary job is to communicate with the Data layer, which can be any RDBMS, set of XML files, text files, and so on. The DAL layer should act as a 'dumb layer' which is used directly by the BLL or any other service layer. The DAL layer should not contain any specific logic in its classes, and it should be used like a "utility" or "helper" class to fetch and store data to and from a data store.

Business logic layer (or the **BLL**) contains the business logic and set of operational rules particular to the application and talks to the data access layer (DAL) to:

- fetch data on which it has to apply rules
- save updated data after applying rules to it
- perform operations and validate data

BLL usually presents the data to the higher Layers (like a GUI layer) after performing business rules on it. This layer may also include error handling, logging, and exception handling strategies, besides encapsulating all the business rules of the project.

UI layer contains the graphical display components and files like ASPX, ASCX, MasterPages, stylesheets and so on. The UI layer usually is the Website or Web Project in the Visual Studio solution for ASP.NET projects.

Most developers confuse the data access code (DAL) as the data layer (DL). The data and data the access layer are different. DAL is the actual code that we use in our applications to connect to a database, and the database itself is actually the data layer (DL).

Here is a sample diagram of how the different layers act:

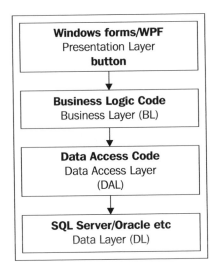

Now in the diagram, if we separate each of the code layers into its own project and class library, then we will have a 4-tier project: Presentation tier, BL tier, DAL tier and DL tier (the physical database).

But with web based applications, we have a built-in 3-tier architecture by default. The presentation tier is the client-side browser (instead of Windows forms), the code (assuming you have web forms, BL, and DAL in one assembly) is the Application tier, and the physical database is the Data tier.

If we break up the web project so that we have the business logic and data access code in one assembly, and the web forms/ascx controls and so on in another, we will have a 4-tier architecture. We can go on like this by breaking each component out into its own tier and introducing further loose coupling. We will see more on how to introduce loose coupling in our projects in the later chapters of this book. For the rest of the book, we will be focusing only on **thin-client** based architectures, that is, web applications in ASP.NET.

We will now see what options we have for how we can break the code into different tier and layers in any Visual Studio web project, and thus define a few models. Here I am assuming that we are breaking the main application into tiers, and not focusing on the database and the presentation (browser) tiers.

Single Tier—Single Layer Model

We will have a single project in our solution, which will have UI, BL and DAL code under a single namespace.

ASP.NET Web Project compiling into a DLL in the /bin folder and under a single namespace: MyApp

No. of project files: 1

No of namespaces: 1

There is no separation of presentation, business logic, and data access code layers. Because we will have only one assembly (or set of assemblies) that cannot be distributed independently, this model would be single tier and single layer. We can use this model for very simple projects, on which only one developer is working and where we are sure there are no major scalability or maintainability issues. For example, a personal guestbook system, small 2 or 3 page web applications, or web sites with mostly static content.

Actually if you make an application based on the above model, it will follow a 3-tier architecture 'overall', if we bring the database and the browser as the other tiers and count them inside the application. This is the reason why I mentioned that for the time being we should forget about the external tiers and focus on how to break the monolithic ASP. NET application into further tiers.

Single Tier—Two Layer Model

In this type of solution, we will still have only one web project, but we will separate the UI code into one namespace, and the BL and DAL into another namespace.

ASP.NET Web Project that has two folders:

- **Code:** This folder will have class files containing business logic and data access code under a single namespace, say MyApp.Code
- **Web:** This folder will have the user controls, ASPX pages, and other presentation-related code under the namespace, say MyApp.Web

Here, as the business logic and data access code are logically separated from the presentation code, we have two layers. However, as all code files would still be compiling into assemblies under a single project's /bin, we will have only one tier. We can use this model for projects that have little or no business logic but need to access a database for content.

Single Tier—Three Layer Model

In this model, we logically break BL and DAL in different namespaces, introducing cleaner code separation.

ASP.NET Web Project that has logical separation between presentation, business logic and data access code:

- All presentation code will be under the MyApp.Web namespace (Layer 1).
- Furthermore, the single project can have two folders:
    ○ Business (Layer 2): for business logic code, with namespace
       MyApp.Code.Business
    ○ DAL (Layer 3): for data access code, with namespace MyApp.
       Code.DAL

Note that it is not necessary to have different folders for the logical separation of code; using different namespaces in different code files will also work fine. We can use this model for a medium-to-large web application where we know that many users won't log in simultaneously. For handling a large number of users, the application needs to be scalable, and to do this we might need to separate BL and DAL code into their own physical assemblies.

Two Tier Model

Here we create two projects, one normal web project for UI code, and another class library project for the BL and DAL code. This will ensure that even if we change the BL or DAL code, we don't need to recompile the web project as we have separate physical assemblies. This setup is more scalable and maintainable than all previous options. Separating code into different assemblies will involve a slight performance hit, but that is negligible considering the flexibility and maintainability benefits we get by having two tiers.

The solution will have:

- ASP.NET Web Project having GUI and presentation code (Tier 1)
- A class library project having business logic and data access coding under a single namespace, MyApp.Code; no separate namespaces for business logic and data access code (Tier 2)

In this case, we still have the BL and DAL code under one namespace, but we can logically separate them further, as shown below.

Two Tier—Two Layer Model

We can further separate the BL and DAL code into their own separate namespaces and class files, so that different developers can work on BL and DAL simultaneously, under a multiteam set up.

The solution will have:

- ASP.NET Web Project having Presentation Layer coding in ASPX and ASCX files, under the namespace, `MyApp.Web` (Tier 1)
- A class library project having two folders (Tier 2):
    - Business: for business logic code, with namespace `MyApp.Code.Business` (Layer 1)
    - DAL: for data access code, with namespace `MyApp.Code.DAL` (Layer 2)

Three Tier Model

If the project is large, with a lot of complicated business logic, then it's more useful to separate the BL and DAL into in their own assemblies so that we can change the BL code without changing the DAL assembly. This makes our application more flexible and loosely-coupled as we can use a different DAL assembly for a different database with the same BL assembly.

The solution will have:

- ASP.NET Web Project having Presentation Layer coding in ASPX and ASCX files, under namespace `MyApp.Web` (Tier 1)
- A class library project having business logic code, with namespace, `MyApp.Code.Business` (Tier 2)
- A class library project DAL for data access code, with namespace, `MyApp.Code.DAL` (Tier 3)

 Once again, if we also bring the Presentation and Database to be a part of the entire application here, the above 3-tier model would become a 5-tier model!

The above structures and layouts show some of the possible ways we can architect our solutions, and also illustrate the differences between layers and tiers. We can have more tiers (n-tier), and can customize our solution with a mix of tiers and layers, according to the project's needs. There is a common misconception among beginner developers that a 3-tier (or n-tier) architecture is the only best model, and many new developers try to blindly follow this model without even giving a second thought to their actual project's needs. As we go from one tier to n-tier, the code complexity increases, and it is better not to go for an n-tier architecture unless the application demands it. For small projects, we can keep things simple and easy.

In the coming chapters we will learn how, why, and which architecture to use (with sample projects), depending on the business needs.

Summary

In this chapter, we learnt the definitions of architecture and design, how they are different from each other and where they fit into our projects. It is very important to understand the different stages of a project life cycle so that we can manage our projects better and mitigate risks early. We also examined the difference between tiers and layers and the different ways we can structure our project using tiers and/or layers. In the coming chapters, we will go deeper into n-tier projects and, with sample applications and code, we will understand the advantages and disadvantages of each option.

2
1-Tier 1-Layer Architecture in ASP.NET

It's time to get our hands dirty with ASP.NET coding! In this chapter, we will understand through the use of examples:

- How every web application is N-tiered by default
- How applications based on classic inline ASP are tightly coupled
- What 1-tier 1-layer architecture is
- Code-behind classes in ASP.NET as another layer in the UI tier
- How Data Source Controls fit into the application architecture of ASP.NET web applications

This chapter is not a guide to how data source controls work, but is rather focused on the architectural aspects of using them and learning about the advantages and disadvantages of data source controls, instead of going into the deep technical details of using them.

Default N-Tier Nature of Web Applications

When working with web applications, a very important concept to grasp is that by its very own nature each web application is distributed and is inherently 2-tier by default (or 3-tier if we include the database as a separate tier). Therefore, it is not possible to have a single-tier (or 1-tier) architecture at all, when dealing with web applications. And as we saw in the last chapter, if we include a database and client browser in our system, then we already have a basic 3-tier application structure.

Let's understand this concept in detail with a sample configuration for a simple ASP.NET web application:

- **Web Server**: A machine running a web server such as IIS, handling all HTTP requests and passing them onto the ASP.NET runtime process. The deployed project files (ASPX, ASCX, DLLs etc) are published on this server.

- **Database Server**: This will be the physical database such as SQL Server, Oracle and so on. It can be on the same machine as the web server or on a separate machine.

- **Client Browser**: This will be the browser that the client is running to view the web application. The browser runs and uses client machine resources.

The example shows a deployment scenario, where we have the web application deployed on machine A, which is running IIS.

This is how the configuration will look:

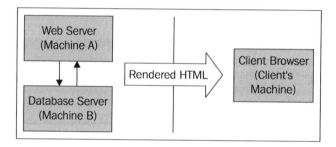

Based on the above diagram, we have a distributed 3-tier architecture with the following tiers:

- **Presentation Tier**: This is the client browser displaying rendered HTML from the web server.

- **Application Tier**: This is machine A, which has the web server running along with the application's UI, business logic, and data access code, all deployed together on the same machine.

- **Data Tier**: This is the database running on machine B. We can also call this a Data Layer.

An important point to note is that in ASP.NET web applications, the presentation tier (browser) is different from the GUI (which is actually the ASPX/ASCX application frontend).

In this chapter, in order to simplify the understanding of application architecture, we will be considering tiers from the application's stand point and therefore ignoring the database (data tier) and client browser (presentation tier). So a single ASP.NET web application, in monolithic terms, is 1-tier. We will see how to break this 1-tier 1-layer web application further into layers and tiers, understanding and analyzing the needs and effects of each step.

Usually, it takes a lot of experience working with different types of architectures to become familiar with the advantages and disadvantages of each approach. A developer who has worked only in 3-tier (or higher) applications may find it very difficult to conceptualize and adapt to a 2-tier approach even though it may be more suitable for his project. He will feel more comfortable in the n-tier based architecture even when it is not required. That is why it is very important to study the 1-tier and 2-tier designs and analyze their pros and cons, to appreciate the usefulness and the real need of breaking it further into multiple tiers and layers.

In this chapter, we will focus on how to break the monolithic default ASP.NET architecture into multiple layers and tiers and see when and where to use this style. We will also see how we can logically break the 2-tier style into different layers for more flexibility and better code management.

Classic ASP Style: Inline Coding

Firstly, we will study the classic inline style of coding, which was the only option available during the good old ASP 3.0 days. This was a mix of interpreted ASP scripts and HTML code. In terms of architecture, there was not much flexibility, although developers used classes to bring some object oriented flavor to the projects, but these were not pure OO classes. Core features such as inheritance were not supported. Moreover, there was lot of effort involved in coding these classes, so most developers preferred to mix coding that was much faster in terms of development time. At a high level, an ASP project configuration would usually follow the given diagram:

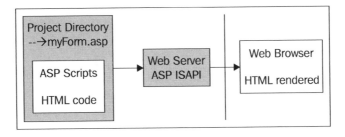

In this diagram, we have ASP script files in the web server directory being processed by ASP **ISAPI (Internet Server Application Programming Interface)** DLL in IIS and rendered in the client browser. ISAPI DLL is a part of IIS itself, and not a separate process such as the ASP.NET runtime engine.

Here is some classic ASP sample code:

```
<%@ language="JScript" %>
<%  var    pubName ="Publisher",
           pageTitle="Publisher Page Title"
                     Response.Write(pubName) %>
<html>
<head><title><% =pageTitle %></title>
</head>
<body>
<div> <% =pubName %>   </div>
</body>
</html>
```

The above ASP code is a simple example which clearly highlights the fact that the pre-ASP net coding style was a messy mixture of HTML and ASP scripts. In this particular style, we had no logical or physical separation of the web application code. It followed a single-layer style—everything was done in the UI layer (which is a part of the application tier, and is different from the presentation tier). With none of the indispensable modern day programming features such as debugging support and IntelliSense, maintenance of such code was nearly a nightmare.

 Programming languages are either compiled or interpreted. ASP code was interpreted line by line, unlike modern higher-level compiled languages such as C++ and C#. Because interpreted code needs to be converted line by line into machine code at runtime, it is usually slower than compiled code, where the entire program is converted into machine instructions in one batch, typically long before any of it is run.

Then came ASP.NET, doing away with the interpreted ASP scripts and introducing a much faster compilation model along with strongly-typed languages such as C# and VB.NET, in addition to numerous other benefits, making it a strong leap from ASP.

Although not recommended, ASP.NET still allows the use of the inline coding model using <script> block constructs for C# and VB.NET code. We don't need to go deeper into inline coding, but here is a simple example of how an ASP 3.0 developer might have intuitively coded a simple project in ASP.NET without using any code-behind.

Sample Project using Inline Code

Let's say we have a simple online guestbook system, which is web-based and developed in ASP.NET. We have a simple web form with a button, and have all coding on the ASPX page itself (inline coding). The system will simply query a Microsoft Access database and return the results to a repeater control.

Here is the ASPX code sample:

```
<%@ Page Language="C#" %>
<%@ Import Namespace="System" %>
<%@ Import Namespace="System.Data" %>
<%@ Import Namespace="System.Data.OleDb" %>
<script language="C#" runat="server">
    private void Page_Load(object sender, EventArgs e)
    {
        //page load coding goes here
    }
    private void btnComments_Click(object sender, EventArgs e)
    {
            LoadComments();
    }
    private void LoadComments()
    {
            string AppPath = System.AppDomain.CurrentDomain.
                            BaseDirectory.ToString();
            string sCon = @"Provider=Microsoft.JET.OLEDB.4.0;
            Data Source=" + AppPath + "/App_Data/Personal.mdb";
            using (OleDbConnection cn = new OleDbConnection(sCon))
            {
                string sQuery = @"SELECT * FROM Guestbook order by
                                EntryDate desc";
                OleDbCommand cmd = new OleDbCommand(sQuery, cn);
                OleDbDataAdapter da = new OleDbDataAdapter(cmd);
                DataSet ds = new DataSet();
                  cn.Open();
                da.Fill(ds);
                rptComments.DataSource = ds;
                rptComments.DataBind();
            }
    }
</script>
```

Note that we have used <script> block for the inline C# code. Now we start the HTML code on the same page (after the </script> ends):

```
<html>
<head runat="server">
    <title>Chapter 2: Inline coding sample in ASPX</title>
</head>
<body>
    <form id="form1" runat="server">
    <div>
        <asp:Button ID="btnComments" runat="server"
                    Text="View All Comments"
                    OnClick="btnComments_Click" />

        <h1> Guestbook Entries</h1>

        <asp:Repeater id="rptComments" runat="server">
        <ItemTemplate>
            Name:   <%# Eval("FullName")%>
                        <br>
            Email:><%# Eval("EmailID")%>
                        <br>
            Website:<%# Eval("Website")%>
                    <br>
                        Dated:          Eval("EntryDate")%>
                    <br>
            Comments:<%# Eval("Comments")%>

        </ItemTemplate>

        </asp:Repeater>

    </div>
    </form>
</body>
</html>
```

In this page, the coding technique used is known as **inline coding,** used in old classic ASP (ASP 3.0) minus the spaghetti mix. Here, the HTML and C# code is mixed in a single file, unlike the default code-behind model used in ASP.NET. But the inline code is separately marked using the <script> tag. This style is basically the 1-tier 1-layer style, with the application tier having the coding logic in the UI layer itself. In classic ASP, there was no easy way to debug such ASP pages, which had both HTML and ASP script mixed up, and the only way to find out if your code was working properly was to use Response.Write() statements throughout the code base, which made debugging a very painstaking and time-consuming process. With improvements in the **IDE**, VS (Visual Studio) could debug such inline code script tags, and VS 2005 upwards also supported IntelliSense in ASPX pages. But mixing code and HTML was still a bad idea for the following reasons:

- **No separation of business logic, data access code, and presentation (HTML)**: It was therefore not possible to have a distributed architecture in the sense that the entire code base was monolithic in nature and could not be physically separated.

- **Code re-use**: Code cannot be re-used in other pages, whereas in code-behind files, we can call methods from a class file in many pages.

- **Source Code Control (SCC) problems**: A developer working on a file will need to block (check-out) the entire file. In the code-behind model, different developers can work on the UI and the code logic, as we have different files for each.

- **Compilation model**: Errors won't be found until the code is executed.

- **Maintenance issue**: Long-term maintenance will be an issue.

There were also some advantages in using this inline model, but the disadvantages above far outweighed any advantages:

- Because we are not using class files, simply updating a page will propagate changes to the server, without causing the users to log off, as no application restart will take place. So we can update without stopping the application, or causing an application restart.

- There can be a slight performance benefit compared to using assemblies, but this will be negligible, as modern day computing power is very fast.

Code-Behind Model: The Second UI Layer

In the above classic ASP style example, we noticed that the code and HTML were separated but still present on the same ASPX page. ASP.NET introduced further separation using the principle of code-behind classes, by pulling all of the code out from the ASPX into a separate class and compiling it to a separate DLL. (Note that a DLL is not really required either, if the developer wishes to deploy the code-behind into the web directory. ASP.NET will compile the code "Just-In-Time" into a temporary DLL, so "pre-compiling into a DLL" is not required either.) This allowed the programmers to debug their applications more efficiently and also introduced further loose coupling in the UI layer, introducing another layer into the above 1-tier architecture.

Here is a diagrammatic representation of the above style:

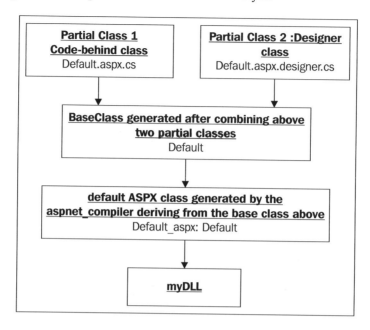

The partial class compilation model was introduced with ASP.NET 2.0. Partial classes help us break up a main class into sibling classes, which can be merged later into one single class by the compiler. We can see that now instead of having a single ASPX file, we have three separate files for a webform—an ASPX file containing HTML UI elements, a code-behind file containing logical code, and an extra designer class file which is auto-generated by the VS and has the declaration of all of the server controls used in the ASPX form. At runtime, the code-behind class is compiled together with the `designer.cs` class (containing protected control declarations), and this merged class is used as the base class for the ASPX form class. This approach helped separate the UI code from the HTML elements, and this logical separation in terms of code-behind classes was the second layer style.

Sample Project using Code-Behind

Here is an example of the same guestbook application being coded using code-behind classes:

```csharp
using System;
using System.Data;
using System.Data.OleDb;
using System.Web;
using System.Web.UI;
using System.Web.UI.WebControls;
using System.Web.UI.HtmlControls;

namespace Chapter2.CodeBehindStyle
{
    public partial class Default : System.Web.UI.Page
    {
        protected void btnComments_Click(object sender, EventArgs e)
        {
            LoadComments();
        }
        /// <summary>
        /// Load all comments from the Access DB
        /// </summary>
        private void LoadComments()
        {
            string AppPath = System.AppDomain.CurrentDomain.
                            BaseDirectory.ToString();
            string sCon = @"Provider=Microsoft.JET.OLEDB.4.0; Data
                    Source=" + AppPath + "/App_Data/Guestbook.mdb";
            using (OleDbConnection cn = new OleDbConnection(sCon))
            {
                string sQuery = @"SELECT * FROM Guestbook order by
                                EntryDate desc";
                OleDbCommand cmd = new OleDbCommand(sQuery, cn);
                OleDbDataAdapter da = new OleDbDataAdapter(cmd);
                DataSet ds = new DataSet();
                cn.Open();
                da.Fill(ds);
                rptComments.DataSource = ds;
                rptComments.DataBind();
            }
        }
    }//end class
}//end namespace
```

In the code above we are simply loading all guestbook entries in the LoadComments() method and binding it to a repeater (rptComments) in the code-behind partial class file.

Here is the ASPX form:

```
<%@ Page Language="C#" AutoEventWireup="true" CodeBehind="Default.
aspx.cs" Inherits="Chapter2.CodeBehindStyle.Default" %>
<html>
<head>
    <title>Chapter 2: Code-behind sample in ASP.NET</title>
</head>
<body>
    <form id="form1" runat="server">
    <div>
        <asp:Button ID="btnComments" runat="server" Text="View All
                      Comments" OnClick="btnComments_Click" />

        <h1>Guestbook Entries</h1>

      <asp:Repeater id="rptComments" runat="server">
          <ItemTemplate>
            Name:    <%# Eval("FullName")%>
                                  <br>
            Email:  <%# Eval("EmailID")%>
                                  <br>
            Website: <%# Eval("Website")%>
                                  <br>
            Dated:   <%# Eval("EntryDate")%>
                                  <br>
            Comments: <%# Eval("Comments")%>
          </ItemTemplate>
      </asp:Repeater>
    </div>
    </form>
</body>
</html>
```

As you can see, we don't have any C# or VB.NET coding in the ASPX pages; all of the managed code is in the code-behind class. Also note that the declaration of any server side control is put in a separate designer.cs file, which is auto-generated after parsing the ASPX markup file. So we have a clean logical separation of the declarative ASPX controls placement (HTML part) and the actual managed code in the code-behind partial classes. Here is a diagrammatic representation of this 1-tier 1-layer style having 2 sub-layers in the main UI layer:

UI Layer

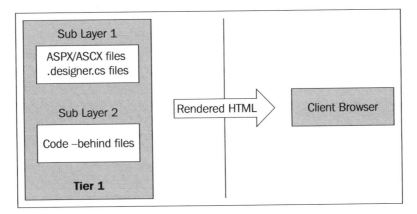

From the given diagram, we can see that we still have one single physical DLL, but the UI code itself is logically separated into two layers—one in the markup code and the other in the code-behind file. Note that, as explained in the beginning of this chapter, this architecture is 1-tier from the application's viewpoint, but overall it is still 3-tier if we consider the client browser as the presentation tier, and the database as the data tier. We are only focusing on the application tier, which houses the UI layer in the above examples.

Limitations of Coding in the UI Layer

Even though we have only one layer, the separation between HTML and UI code, using code-behind files, helps the web designers to work independently of the developers. Both have separate files to work on. This is a recommended practice, as mixing UI markup with logical UI processing code can lead to a spaghetti mixture. Besides this furthermore, the style is more object-oriented than inline coding as we write code in code-behind classes instead of writing it in interpreted free-style blocks as in classic ASP. So code-behind helps us manage and maintain our code in the long run, when compared to inline coding.

However, note that even though we have separated the code into two layers, both of these layers actually belong to the UI layer. Even if we are putting data access or business logic code in the code-behind files, we are still mixing the UI layer with non-UI code, which is not recommended for commercial scalable applications. In the coming chapters you will learn how to further use layers and tiers to make your application more scalable.

But if your project is small, for example, a 4–5 page website for personal use or a small data entry website which is not intended to grow in size, complexity, or user base, and where there is no future need to scale it up, then putting the data access code in the code-behind files is acceptable. Remember — "if it ain't broke, then don't fix it". There is no need to complicate a simple web application if there is no actual requirement to justify doing so. Designing scalable solutions from the start is a good approach, but that does not mean we need to start over-architecting every website we work on without thinking twice about its real use and application. Furthermore, budget constraints sometimes might not allow us to adopt a fully-fledged N-tier scalable solution because the project is either too small or there is no scope for it to grow further, and therefore the project stakeholders might not want to spend too much on its development because building a scalable architecture takes time and will not make economic sense for a small project.

Next, we will learn about Data Source Controls, and how we can put them to best use for small projects.

Data Source Controls

With further refinements to ASP.NET 2.0, Microsoft has added many out-of-the-box controls (apart from the standard web control library). Some of the most useful controls are Data Source Controls, complimenting the feature-rich web server controls such as the GridView and the DetailsView. These controls have made it possible to create applications without writing even a single line of data access code. Now it is possible to create web applications within a short timespan, doing away with many lines of routine data access code.

With Data Source Controls, we can use SQL queries as well as stored procedures, and write custom code too. Although we won't go deep into the details of how to use controls, as there are many freely-available online resources and articles on this subject, we will see how using these controls affects the overall architecture, when to use them and what their disadvantages are.

A Sample Project using Inbuilt Data Source Controls

Let's start with our good old guestbook application! This time we will see how to insert data using data controls with little or no programming. Here is how the form looks:

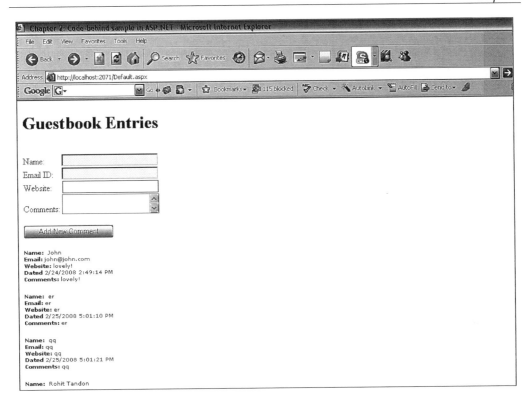

Open the `default.aspx` form and drag an access Data Source control onto it. Put a few textbox controls on the web form, as this time we will perform insert operations without writing any SQL code. Now, we need to set the insert parameters declaratively:

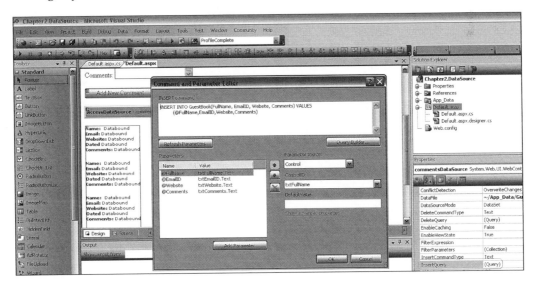

This is how the code-behind will now look:

```
using System;
using System.Data;
using System.Data.OleDb;
using System.Configuration;
using System.Collections;
using System.Web;
using System.Web.UI;
using System.Web.UI.WebControls;
using System.Web.UI.HtmlControls;
namespace Chapter2.DataSource
{
    public partial class Default : System.Web.UI.Page
    {
        protected void btnAddComment_Click(object sender, EventArgs e)
        {
            commentsDataSource.Insert();
            rptComments.DataBind();
        }
    }//end class
}//end namespace
```

As we can see, there is absolutely no data access code except calling the insert method of the data control. Here is the ASPX where we had set the insert parameters declaratively using Visual Studio:

```
<%@ Page Language="C#" AutoEventWireup="true" CodeBehind="Default.
aspx.cs" Inherits="Chapter2.DataSource.Default" %>
<html>
<head id="Head1" runat="server">
    <title>Chapter 2: Data source control sample in ASP.NET</title>
</head>
<body>
    <form id="form1" runat="server">
    <div>
         <h1>
        Guestbook Entries</h1>

        <br />
        Name:
        <asp:TextBox ID="txtFullName" runat="server" Width="174px">
                                            </asp:TextBox>
        Email ID:
        <asp:TextBox ID="txtEmailID" runat="server" Width="174px">
                                            </asp:TextBox><br />
```

```
Website:
<asp:TextBox ID="txtWebsite" runat="server" Width="173px">
                                          </asp:TextBox><br />

Comments:
<asp:TextBox ID="txtComments" runat=
        "server" TextMode="MultiLine"></asp:TextBox><br />
<br />
<asp:Button ID="btnAddComment" runat="server" Text=
  "Add New Comment" OnClick="btnAddComment_Click" /><br />
<br />
<asp:AccessDataSource ID="commentsDataSource" runat=
                    "server" DataFile="~/App_Data/Guestbook.mdb"
  SelectCommand="SELECT * FROM [GuestBook]"
  InsertCommand="INSERT INTO GuestBook(FullName,
            EmailID, Website, Comments) VALUES
  (@FullName,EmailID,Website,Comments)">
      <InsertParameters>
          <asp:ControlParameter Name="@FullName"
              ControlID="txtFullName" PropertyName="Text" />
          <asp:ControlParameter Name="@EmailID"
              ControlID="txtEmailID" PropertyName="Text" />
          <asp:ControlParameter Name="@Website"
              ControlID="txtWebsite" PropertyName="Text" />
          <asp:ControlParameter Name="@Comments"
              ControlID="txtComments" PropertyName="Text" />
      </InsertParameters>
  </asp:AccessDataSource>

<asp:Repeater id="rptComments" runat="server" DataSourceID=
                                "commentsDataSource">
              <ItemTemplate>
                      Name:<%# Eval("FullName")%>
                      <br>
                      Email:<%# Eval("EmailID")%>
                      <br>
                      Website: <%# Eval("Website")%>
                      <br>
                      Dated: <%# Eval("EntryDate")%>
                      <br>
                      Comments:<%# Eval("Comments")%>
                       </ItemTemplate>
                  </asp:Repeater>
    </div>
  </form>
</body>
</html>
```

Set the mode of the **DataSourceMode** property to **DataReader** instead of **Dataset** for better performance.

The use of Data Source Controls can cut down the use of data access code and shorten the development time. In the above example, we inserted the data without writing any code. Similarly, we can perform updates, deletes, and other CRUD operations, and use data controls with other controls such as the GridView and the DetailsView.

The Data Source Controls wrap the data access code logic, and use declarative markup in the ASPX page. So using these controls means that we are strongly coupling the GUI markup with the data access code, which may be fine for small applications such as a personal website, but should not be used for any commercial medium-to-large web applications.

When using data controls, the architecture is still 1-tier, but the layers change. Instead of using data fetching, and binding code in the code-behind classes, we simply use the declarative markup of Data Source Controls. This is good for turning out applications quickly, but we lose finer control over data-access.

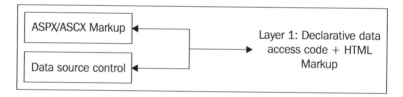

We have all of the code, as well as the markup, in the ASPX page. As mentioned earlier, having the data access code in the GUI violates the basic principle of code separation—the GUI should be independent of the business logic or data access code. Therefore, data controls are useful for small projects only. Here is a list of the advantages and disadvantages of using data controls in web projects:

Advantages:

- Cuts down heavily on coding and saves cost and development time.
- Declarative markup allows changes to propagate on the server without re-compiling the site.
- Ready support for data-bound controls such as GridView, DetailsView, and DataList.

Disadvantages:

- Highly-coupled GUI and data access code.

- Only good for small applications with no business logic.

- Scalability issues—if the project grows big, then performance will be affected.

- Not efficient when dealing with complex hierarchical result-sets.

- Because they abstract data access operations, they are not very flexible and may present problems when dealing with customized data.

A simple guestbook application for a personal website is one such case warranting the use of data controls. Such applications have quick turn-around time, and one can build a working application in a matter of few days. If we do not use Data Source Controls, then we can directly write custom data access code in the code-behind file. Although we will be putting non-UI related code in the UI layer even then, we will have more flexibility as we can write custom SQL statements and modify data at runtime, which is quite difficult to do using Data Source Controls.

To overcome the disadvantages of data controls, Microsoft introduced Object Data Source control, to support business objects, and business logic code and the N-tier architecture. We will learn more about object Data Source Controls in the next chapter.

Summary

In this chapter, we examined how web applications inherently follow a 3-tier client-server model, and how a 1-tier architecture can be used for simple applications in ASP.NET. Then we learned how we can logically partition this basic 1-tier 1-layer architectural style into two sub-layers, using code-behind files. We also studied how declarative code-less programming using new Data Source Controls follows a single-layer style.

In a nutshell:

- Classic inline coding should not be used unless absolutely necessary. One case supporting it would be a project that mixes classic ASP and ASP.NET, or a project already built using this style of coding.

- Data Source Controls (except Object Data Source) are only good for small projects which will never need to be scaled up in the future. For commercial-level projects, it's very important to logically break the code into layers.

- The code-behind style is much more flexible, object-oriented, and scalable for commercial projects. We can break these layers further, into more layers, for better code management and maintainability, as we will see in the coming chapters of this book.

We saw that although we have separated the HTML and code elements, all of the code is still in a single code-behind class (1-tier 1-layer style). For a decently-sized commercial application, having data access and business logic code in the same code-behind file is not a good practice, as code-behind belongs to the UI layer. For further loose coupling, the UI layer should handle only the UI events and should not contain data access or any business logic code. In the coming chapters, we will learn how to break up this 1-tier 1-layer architecture into an n-tier and n-layer architecture so that we can achieve a higher degree of loose coupling, and make our applications more scalable and robust.

3

ER Diagrams, Domain Model, and N-Layer Architecture

In the last chapter, we saw the basic layering of the monolithic 1-tier 1-layer architectural style in action, with the UI layer having code-behind classes as the sub-layer. This 1-tier 1-layer architecture is the default style in ASP.NET and Visual Studio 2005/2008. To overcome the limitations of this style, we can further break the application code into n-layers, where the number "n" actually depends on the project requirements.

In this chapter we will:

- Learn the 2-layer style
- Understand ER diagrams
- Understand what a domain model is, and what UML relationships are
- Learn the 3-layer style
- Learn about object data source controls

Let's revisit the 1-tier ASP.NET application configuration described in the last chapter.

 Note that the application as a whole including database and client browser is three tier.

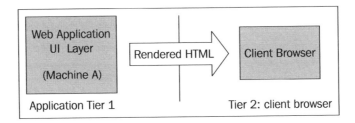

As mentioned in the last chapter, we can call this 1-tier architecture a 3-tier architecture if we include the browser and database (if used). For the rest of this chapter we will ignore the database and browser as separate tiers so that we can focus on how to divide the main ASP.NET application layers logically, using the n-layer pattern to its best use.

We will first try to separate the data access and logical code into their own separate layers and see how we can introduce flexibility and re-usability into our solution. We will understand this with a sample project. Before we go ahead into the technical details and code, we will first learn about two important terms: ER Diagram and Domain Model, and how they help us in getting a good understanding of the application we need to develop.

Entity-Relationship Diagram

Entity-Relationship diagrams, or ER diagrams in short, are graphical representations depicting relationships between different entities in a system. We humans understand and remember pictures or images more easily than textual information. When we first start to understand a project we need to see how different entities in the project relate to each other. ER diagrams help us achieve that goal by graphically describing the relationships.

 An entity can be thought of as an object in a system that can be identified uniquely. An entity can have attributes; an attribute is simply a property we can associate with an entity. For example, a Car entity can have the following attributes: EngineCapacity, NumberofGears, SeatingCapacity, Mileage, and so on. So attributes are basically fields holding data to indentify an entity. Attributes cannot exist without an entity.

Let us understand ER diagrams in detail with a simple e-commerce example: a very basic Order Management System. We will be building a simple web based system to track customer's orders, and manage customers and products. To simplify the learning curve, we will use this example regularly in the coming chapters, to see how different architectural styles shape the solution differently, and how we can move towards a more scalable n-tier system.

To start with, let us list the basic entities for our simplified Order Management System (OMS):

- **Customer**: A person who can place Orders to buy Products.
- **Order**: An order placed by a Customer. There can be multiple Products bought by a Customer in one Order.

- **Product**: A Product is an object that can be purchased by a Customer.

- **Category**: Category of a Product. A Category can have multiple Products, and a Product can belong to many Categories. For example, a mixer-grinder can be under the Electronic Gadgets category as well as in Home Appliances.

- **OrderLineItem**: An Order can be for multiple Products. Each individual Product in an order will be encapsulated by an OrderLineItem. So an Order can have multiple OrderLineItems.

Now, let us picture the relationship between the core business entities is defined using an Entity-Relationship diagram. Our ER diagram will show the relational associations between the entities from a database's perspective. So it is more of a relational model and will not show any of the object-oriented associations (for which we will use the Domain Model in the later sections of this chapter). In an ER diagram, we show entities using rectangular boxes, the relationships between entities using diamond boxes and attributes using oval boxes, as shown below:

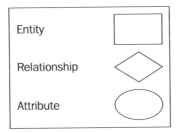

The purpose of using such shapes is to make the ER diagram clear and concise, depicting the relational model as closely as possible without using long sentences or text. So the Customer entity with some of the basic attributes can be depicted in an ER diagram as follows:

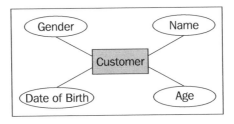

Now, let us create an ER diagram for our Order Management System. For the sake of simplicity, we will not list the attributes of the entities involved.

Here is how the ER diagram looks:

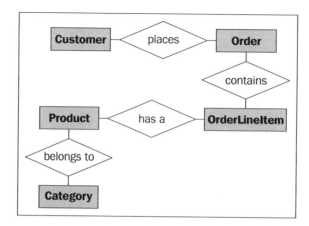

The above ER diagram depicts the relationships between the OMS entities but is still incomplete as the relationships do not show how the entities are quantitatively related to each other. We will now look at how to quantify relationships using degree and cardinality.

Degree and Cardinality of a Relationship

The relationships in an ER diagram can also have a *degree*. A degree specifies the multiplicity of a relationship. In simpler terms, it refers to the number of entities involved in a relationship. All relationships in an OMS ER diagram have a degree of two, also called binary relationships. For example, in Customer-Order relationships only two entities are involved — Customer and Order; so it's a two degree relationship. Most relationships you come across would be binary.

Another term associated with a relationship is cardinality. The cardinality of a relationship identifies the number of instances of entities involved in that particular relationship. For example, an Order can have multiple OrderLineItems, which means the cardinality of the relationship between Order and OrderLineItem is one-to-many. The three commonly-used cardinalities of a relationship are:

- **One-to-one**: Depicted as 1:1

    Example: One OrderLineItem can have only one Product; so the OrderLineItem and Product entities share a one-to-one relationship

- **One-to-many**: Depicted as 1:n

    Example: One customer can place multiple orders, so the Customer and Order entities share a one-to-many relationship

- **Many-to-many**: Depicted as n:m

  Example: One Product can be included in multiple Categories and one Category can contain multiple Products; therefore the Product and Category entities share a many-to-many relationship

After adding the cardinality of the relationships to our ER diagram, here is how it will look:

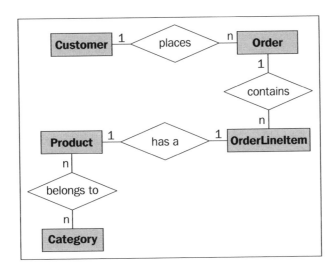

This basic ER diagrams tells us a lot about how the different entities in the system are related to each other, and can help new programmers to quickly understand the logic and the relationships of the system they are working on. Each entity will be a unique table in the database.

OMS Project using 2-Layer

We know that the default coding style in ASP.NET 2.0 already supports the 1-tier 1-layer style, with two sub-layers in the main UI layer as follows:

- Designer code files: ASPX markup files
- Code behind files: Files containing C# or VB.NET code

Because both of these layers contain the UI code, we can include them as a part of the UI layer. These two layers help us to separate the markup and the code from each other. However, it is still not advisable to have logical code, such as data access or business logic, directly in these code-behind files.

Now, one way to create an ASP.NET web application for our Order Management System (OMS) in just one layer is by using a DataSet (or DataReader) to fill the front-end UI elements directly in the code-behind classes. This will involve writing data access code in the UI layer (code-behind), and will tightly bind this UI layer with the data access logic, making the application rigid (inflexible), harder to maintain, and less scalable. We have already seen this approach in the guestbook example in Chapter 2 (2-layered systems), and we know the drawbacks of this approach.

In order to have greater flexibility, and to keep the UI layer completely independent of the data access and business logic code, we need to put these elements in separate files. So we will now try and introduce some loose-coupling by following a 2-layer approach this time. What we will do is, write all data access code in separate class files instead of using the code-behind files of the UI layer. This will make the UI layer independent of the data-access code.

 We are assuming that we do not have any specific business logic code at this point, or else we would have put that under another layer with its own namespace, making it a 3-layered architecture. We will examine this in the upcoming sections of this chapter.

Sample Project

Let us see how we can move from this 1-tier 1-layer style to a 1-tier 2-layer style. Using the ER diagram above as reference, we can create a 2-Layer architecture for our OMS with these layers:

- UI-layer with ASPX and code-behind classes
- Data access classes under a different namespace but in the same project

So let's start with a new VS 2008 project. We will create a new ASP.NET Web Project in C#, and add a new web form, `ProductList.aspx`, which will simply display a list of all the products using a Repeater control. The purpose of this project is to show how we can logically break up the UI layer further by separating the data access code into another class file.

The following is the ASPX markup of the ProductList page (unnecessary elements and tags have been removed to keep things simple):

```
<asp:Repeater ID="prodRepeater" runat="server">
    <ItemTemplate>
        Product Code:  <%# Eval("Code")%>
            <br>
        Name:          <%# Eval("Name")%>
```

```
                    <br>
        Unit Price:   $<%# Eval("UnitPrice")%>
                    <br>
    </ItemTemplate>
</asp:Repeater>
```

In this ASPX file, we only have a Repeater control, which we will bind with the data in the code-behind file.

Here is the code in the `ProductList.aspx.cs` code-behind file:

```
namespace OMS
{
public partial class _Default : System.Web.UI.Page
    {
        /// <summary>
        /// Page Load method
        /// </summary>
        /// <param name="sender"></param>
        /// <param name="e"></param>
        protected void Page_Load(object sender, EventArgs e)
        {
            DataTable dt = DAL.GetAllProducts();
            prodRepeater.DataSource = dt;
            prodRepeater.DataBind();
        }
    }//end class
}//end namespace
```

Note that we don't have any data access code in the code-behind sample above. We are just calling the `GetAllProducts()` method, which has all of data access code wrapped in a different class named DAL. As we saw in the last section of Chapter 1, we can logically separate out the code, by using different namespaces to achieve code re-use and greater architectural flexibility. So we created a new class named DAL under a different namespace from the UI layer code files. Here is the DAL code:

```
namespace OMS.Code
{
    public class DAL
    {
        /// <summary>
        /// Load all comments from the Access DB
        /// </summary>
        public static DataTable GetAllProducts()
        {
            string sCon = ConfigurationManager.ConnectionStrings[0].
```

```
ConnectionString;
        using (SqlConnection cn = new SqlConnection(sCon))
        {
            string sQuery = @"SELECT * FROM OMS_Product";
            SqlCommand cmd = new SqlCommand(sQuery, cn);
            SqlDataAdapter da = new SqlDataAdapter(cmd);
            DataSet ds = new DataSet();
            cn.Open();
            da.Fill(ds);
            return ds.Tables[0];
        }
    }
}//end class
}//end namespace
```

So we have separated the data access code in a new logical layer, using a separate namespace, OMS.Code, and using a new class. Now, if we want to, we can re-use the same code in the other pages as well. Furthermore, methods to add and edit a product can be defined in this class and then used in the UI layer. This allows multiple developers to work on the DAL and UI layers simultaneously.

Even though we have a logical separation of the code in this 2-layer sample architecture, we are still not using real Object Oriented Programming (OOP). All of the Object-Oriented Programming we have used so far has been the default structure the .NET framework has provided, such as the Page class, and so on.

When a project grows big in size as well as complexity, using the 2-layer model discussed above can become cumbersome and cause scalability and flexibility issues. If the project grows in complexity, then we will be putting all of the business logic code in either the DAL or the UI layer. This business logic code includes business rules. For example, if the customer orders a certain number of products in one order, he gets a certain level of discount. If we code such business rules in the UI layer, then if the rules change we need to change the UI as well, which is not ideal, especially in cases where we can have multiple UIs for the same code, for example one normal web browser UI and another mobile-based UI.

We also cannot put business logic code in the DAL layer because the DAL layer should only contain data access code which should not be mixed with any kind of business processing logic. In fact the DAL layer should be quite "dumb"–there should be no "logic" inside it because it is mostly a utility layer which only needs to put data in and pull data out from a data store.

To make our applications more scalable and to reap the benefit of OOP, we need to create objects, and wrap business behavior in their methods. This is where the Domain Model comes into the picture.

Domain Model using UML

The domain model is a more object-oriented way of indicating the relationships between different objects in the context of the business logic of the application. It is similar to the ER diagram. But instead of merely showing the relationships between the entities involved, it graphically reflects how these entities relate to each other in an object-oriented fashion. On the other hand, an ER diagram is only focused from a relational perspective.

Unified Modeling Language, or UML in short, is a graphical language used to describe object-oriented designs for software systems. UML is quite a vast language, but we will focus more on class diagrams and UML relationships to represent our domain model. Class diagrams are widely used in every object-oriented system to describe the different types of internal relationships between the different business entities.

Before going for a 3-layer object-oriented system, we need to create a domain model of the system. So we need to put all of the business code into separate logical structures and start creating a domain model, in order to understand the different business entities involved.

For this, we need to "organize" the code by breaking it down into logical entities, which we call objects, and create relationships between them. The resulting set of objects with relationships defined between them would be known as the domain model of the application. It is so called because this model illustrates how different entities in the application domain would interact with each other.

We use the following shapes in our class diagram:

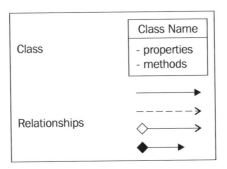

We will learn in detail what each figure represents, and how to create a domain model using them.

Class Diagram

A class diagram simply represents how different entities are related to each other in an object-oriented system. Class diagrams are different from ER diagrams because class diagrams deal with relationships in an object-oriented manner, showing inheritance, interfaces and so on, whereas an ER diagram can only depict relational models (for Relational Database Management Systems, or RDBMSs).

In order to create a class diagram for our OMS, let us highlight the major entities in our OMS in terms of domain classes:

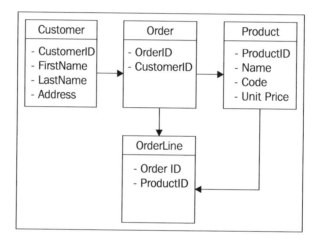

The rectangular boxes denote the entities (or classes) with the class name in the header and the attributes (or fields) below it. The arrows define relationships between entities. These relationships can be of different types and are depicted differently using different arrow styles.

Broadly speaking, we can place class relationships into these categories:

- Dependency relationship
- Association
- Generalization
- Realization

Let's explore each of these UML relationships in detail.

UML Relationships

In an ER diagram for two entities A and B, we can show only one type of relationship–a Relational relationship–which means that entity A is somehow related to entity B. But in a class diagram, the relationships can be further divided on the basis of object-oriented principles such as inheritance, association, and so on. The following sections describe the main UML relationships used in a class diagram.

Dependency Relationship

A **Dependency** exists between two elements if changes to one element will affect the other. A dependency relationship is the simplest relationship of all, and means that Entity 1 depends on Entity 2 in such a way that any change in entity 2 might break entity 1. This is a one-way relationship only — changes in entity 1 will not affect entity 2 in any manner. Dependency relationships are represented by a broken (dashed) line with an "empty" arrow (--->). The direction of this arrow flows to the entity that is dependent on the entity that the arrow flows from.

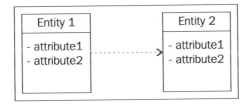

A simple example would be:

```
public class Entity1
{
    public void MethodX (Entity2 en)
    {
        // . . .
    }
    public void MethodY ()
    {
        Entity2 en2 = new Entity2();
        // . . .
    }
}
```

In the above pseudo code, Entity2 is used in Entity1 first as a method parameter and secondly inside `MethodY()` as a local variable. Both of these cases show a dependency relationship.

An important point about dependency relationships relates to the state of the objects involved. The state of Entity2 is not related to the state of Entity-1, as Entity2 is not a member of the Entity1 class. It is only used in the methods as local variable.

Association Relationship

An **Association** shows the relationship between instances of classes. An association is similar to a dependency except that it specifies the relationship in a stricter form. An association means that instead of Entity2 being used in Entity1 as a local variable, it would be a global variable instead, which can be a private, public, or protected class member. In its basic form, it is represented by a solid arrow (instead of dashed as in a dependency relationship).

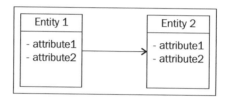

```
public class Order   //entity1
{
   private Customer _customer;
   public Customer GetCustomer ()
   {
      return _customer;
   }
}
```

In the above pseudo code, the Customer object is a part of the Order class—a private member in this case. This means that the Customer object forms a part of the state of the Order. If you have an Order object, you can easily identify the Customer associated with it. This is not possible in a dependency. Hence, the association is a stronger form of dependency.

An Association relationship can be divided further into two separate relationships, based on the state of the aggregated object in the dependent class.

Aggregation

An **Aggregation** relationship depicts a classifier as a part of, or as subordinate to, another classifier. For example, if Entity1 goes out of scope, it does not mean that Entity2 has to go out of scope too. That is, the lifetime of Entity2 is not necessarily controlled by Entity1. An aggregation is represented by a straight arrow, with an empty diamond at the tail, as shown in the following figure:

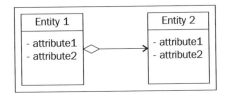

So, in our example, Entity2 is a part of (or subordinate to) Entity 1. If you destroy the parent class (Entity 1) in an aggregation (weak) relationship, the child class (Entity 2) can survive on its own.

Let's understand aggregations by using our example of the Order Management System. Consider the OrderLine and Product classes. An OrderLine can have multiple quantities of one Product. If an OrderLine is destroyed, it does not mean that we delete the Product as well. A Product can exist independently of the OrderLine object. Here is the relationship diagram between OrderLine and Product classes:

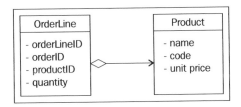

In the diagram, we can see an Aggregation relationship between OrderLine and Product classes. Put simply, the above diagram states that if an order is cancelled, all of the products will not be destroyed; they will only be "de-associated" from that particular order.

Composition

A **Composition** is exactly like Aggregation except that the lifetime of the 'part' is controlled by the 'whole'. For example: You have a 'student' who has a 'schedule'. If you destroy the student, the schedule will cease to exist.

In this case, the associated entity is destroyed when the parent entity goes out of scope. Composition is represented by a straight arrow with a solid diamond at the tail, as shown below.

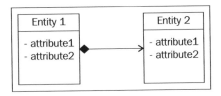

In our case, Entity-2 is controlled by Entity-1. If Entity 1 is destroyed in a composition (strong) relationship, Entity-2 is destroyed as well.

Let's understand compositions by using our example of the Order Management System. Consider the Customer and Order classes. A Customer can have one or more orders, and an Order can have one or more Products (in order lines). An Order object cannot exist on its own without a Customer. So the following Composition indicates that if a Customer object goes out of scope, the Orders associated with that Customer go out of scope too.

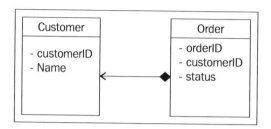

Generalization Relationship

Inheritance is a very widely known and common feature of OOP. In UML, inheritance is depicted using generalization relationships, depicted by a straight arrow with a hollow arrowhead (triangle) at one end. A generalization relationship (also known as a "is-a" relationship) implies that a specialized (child) class is based on a general (parent) class.

Here is a diagram illustrating this:

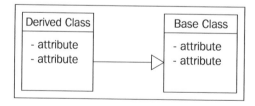

Here, we can see that the arrow points in the direction of the base class. In our Order Management System, we can have a base class for all customers; we can call it Person class so that we have other classes derived from it, such as Customer, CSR (Customer Sales Representative), and so on.

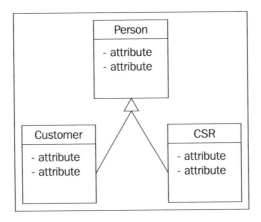

Realization Relationship

Realization is similar to generalization but depicts the relationship between an interface and a class implementing that interface. In UML, realization is depicted with a dashed arrow with a hollow arrowhead (triangle) at one end. A realization relationship exists between the two classes when one of them must realize, or implement, the behavior specified by the other.

For example, a realization relationship connects an interface to an implementing class. The interface specifies the behaviors, and the implementing class implements the behaviors. Here is a diagram illustrating this:

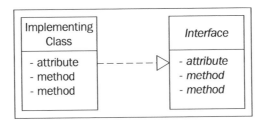

Here, we can see that the arrow points in the direction of the interface. Note that the italicized text in entities that are interfaces. It is UML convention to italicize interfaces.

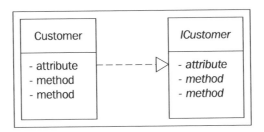

Multiplicity

Multiplicity quantifies the relationship between two entities. Multiplicity is closely related to the cardinality of a relationship, which we learned about earlier when discussing ER diagram. Multiplicity indicates how many instances of classes (objects) are related to each other in a UML relationship. The following is a list of different multiplicities we can have between two entities in a class diagram:

- **One-to-one**: For example, one OrderLine object can have only one product. This is depicted as follows:

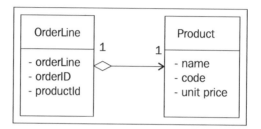

  Note how we show a 1:1 multiplicity using the number "1" at the end points of the aggregation relationship.

- **One-to-many**: For example, a customer can have many orders. This is depicted as follows:

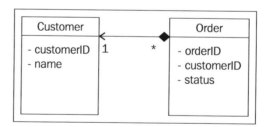

  Note the text "1" and "*" near the entities; these are multiplicity indicators. In the above example, the multiplicity indicates that one (1) customer can have multiple orders (*). We depict "many" using a "*" (asterisk) symbol.

The relationship between Order and OrderLine objects is the same. An order can have multiple products; each product will be shown in a separate line (called as OrderLine) in the Order. So there can be one or more order lines for a single order, as shown here:

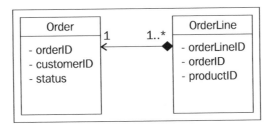

The above diagram confirms that for each order, there will be one or more order lines. We can't use 0..* here in place of 1..* because each order will have atleast one product in it (as one order line item).

Also, if an order gets cancelled (destroyed), then all order lines will be destroyed. It doesn't make sense to have order lines that are not a part of any order — hence the composition.

- **Many-to-many**: A Product can belong to multiple Categories, and a Category object can include multiple Product objects. To depict such many-to-many relationships, we use asterisk at both ends of the relationship arrow, as shown here:

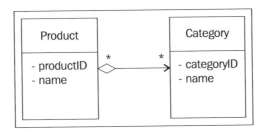

Also note the aggregation relationship between the Product and the Category, because both can exist independently of each other.

So, now, we can combine all of the above diagrams and create a simple class diagram with all of the relationships and multiplicities for our OMS. Here is the combined UML class diagram for our sample application:

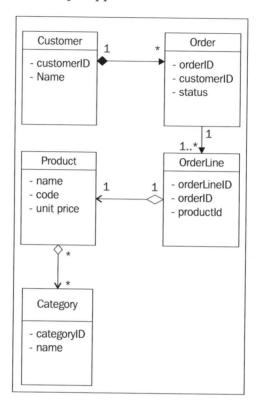

So we have a very simple domain model of a simple Order Management System. Now, based on the above classes, let's look at how we can convert this domain model to code by creating a 1-tier 3-layer architecture based web application.

1-tier 3-layer Architecture using a Domain Model

Based on the above class diagram, we will create a new simple 3-layered application using the entities defined in the above domain model. We will create a new ASP.NET Web Project in VS. This time, you should create two new folders inside your root web folder (using the **Add New Folder** option in VS):

- **BL**: This folder will contain all of the business logic domain classes
- **DAL**: This folder will contain the data access code files (for each entity)

Layer 1: Data Access Layer (DAL)

First, we will create a DAL class for each entity. We will name each DAL class using this naming pattern: EntityDAL. Let us see the CustomerDAL class:

```
using DomainModel.BL;
namespace DomainModel.DAL
{
    public class CustomerDAL
    {
        public static void AddCustomer(Customer cs)
        {
            using (SqlConnection con =
                new SqlConnection(SQLHelper.GetConnectionString()))
            {
                SqlParameter[] par = new SqlParameter[4];
                par[0] = new SqlParameter("@customerID", cs.ID);
                par[0].Direction = ParameterDirection.Output;
                par[1] = new SqlParameter("@name", cs.Name);
                par[2] = new SqlParameter("@address", cs.Address);
                par[3] = new SqlParameter(
                        "@phoneNo", cs.PhoneNumber);
                int rowNo = SQLHelper.ExecuteNonQuery(
                        con, CommandType.StoredProcedure,
                        "OMS_AddCustomer", par);
                cs.ID = Convert.ToInt32(par[0].Value);
            }
        }
        public static void DeleteCustomer(int customerID)
        {
            using (SqlConnection con =
            new SqlConnection(SQLHelper.GetConnectionString()))
            {
                SqlParameter[] par = new SqlParameter[1];
                par[0] = new SqlParameter("@customerID", customerID);
                int rowNo = SQLHelper.ExecuteNonQuery(
                con, CommandType.StoredProcedure,
                "OMS_DeleteCustomer", par);
            }
        }
        public static void UpdateCustomer(Customer cs)
        {
            using (SqlConnection con = new
            SqlConnection(SQLHelper.GetConnectionString()))
            {
                SqlParameter[] par = new SqlParameter[4];
```

```
                par[0] = new SqlParameter("@customerID", cs.ID);
                par[1] = new SqlParameter("@address", cs.Address);
                par[2] = new SqlParameter("@name", cs.Name);
                par[3] = new SqlParameter(
                        "@phoneNo", cs.PhoneNumber);
                int rowNo = SQLHelper.ExecuteNonQuery(
                        con, CommandType.StoredProcedure,
                        "OMS_UpdateCustomer", par);
            }
        }
        public static void GetCustomer(Customer cs)
        {
            using (SqlConnection con =
                new SqlConnection(SQLHelper.GetConnectionString()))
            {
                SqlParameter[] par = new SqlParameter[1];
                par[0] = new SqlParameter("@customerID", customerID);
                using (SqlDataReader dr =
                        SQLHelper.ExecuteReader(con,
                        CommandType.StoredProcedure,
                        "OMS_GetCustomer", par))
                {
                    c = new Customer();
                    while (dr.Read())
                    {
                        c.Name =
                        SQLHelper.CheckStringNull(dr["Name"]);
                        c.PhoneNumber =
                        SQLHelper.CheckStringNull(dr["PhoneNo"]);
                        c.Address =
                        SQLHelper.CheckStringNull(dr["Address"]);
                        c.ID = SQLHelper.CheckIntNull(dr["ID"]);
                    }
                }
            }
        }
        public static List<Customer> GetAllCustomers()
        {
            List<Customer> cuList = new List<Customer>();
            using (SqlConnection con =
                new SqlConnection(SQLHelper.GetConnectionString()))
            {
                using (SqlDataReader dr =
                SQLHelper.ExecuteReader(con,CommandType.
                StoredProcedure,"OMS_GetAllCustomer"))
                {
```

```
                while (dr.Read())
                {
                    Customer customer = new Customer();
                    customer.Name =
                    SQLHelper.CheckStringNull(dr["Name"]);
                    customer.PhoneNumber =
                    SQLHelper.CheckStringNull(dr["PhoneNo"]);
                    customer.Address =
                    SQLHelper.CheckStringNull(dr["Address"]);
                    customer.ID =
                    SQLHelper.CheckIntNull(dr["ID"]);
                    cuList.Add(customer);
                }
            }
        }
        return cuList;
    }
}//end class
}
```

Here, we have used the `SqlHelper` class, which contains generic data access utility methods, so that we can avoid code repletion.

Layer 2: Business Layer (BL)

Next, we will create classes for each of the domain entities. We will put all of these classes under the new BL folder with this namespace: `DomainModel.BL`. Create a new C# class file named `Customer.cs` under the BL folder. Here is the first Customer class:

```
using DomainModel.DAL;
namespace DomainModel.BL
{
    public class Customer
    {
        private int _ID;
        private string _name;
        private string _address;
        private string _phoneNumber;
        private List<Customer> _customerCollection;
        public int ID
        {
            get { return _ID; }
            set { _ID = value; }
        }
```

```csharp
        public string Name
        {
            get { return _name; }
            set { _name = value; }
        }
        public string Address
        {
            get { return _address; }
            set { _address = value; }
        }
        public string PhoneNumber
        {
            get { return _phoneNumber; }
            set { _phoneNumber = value; }
        }
        public List<Customer> CustomerCollection
        {
            get { return _customerCollection; }
            set { _customerCollection = value; }
        }
        public void Add()
        {
            CustomerDAL.AddCustomer(this);
        }
        public void Delete(int customerID)
        {
            CustomerDAL.DeleteCustomer(this.ID);
        }
        public void Update()
        {
            CustomerDAL.UpdateCustomer(this);
        }
        public  void Load()
        {
            CustomerDAL.GetCustomer(this.ID);
        }
       public void GetAll()
        {
            this.CustomerCollection = CustomerDAL.GetAllCustomers();
        }
    }//end class
}//end namespace
```

The `CustomerDAL` class is pretty simple: we are fetching the data from the database using data readers, and performing all data related operations using the Customer business object. This Customer class is defined in the `Customer.cs` class we created earlier. This BL class is calling DAL methods, so it needs a reference to the DAL namespace (using `DomainModel.DAL`). Similarly, the DAL class we created earlier used Customer business objects. That's why it also needed the BL namespace.

We are using generics to create a collection of Customer objects. The BL communicates with DAL to get the data and perform updates. Now, we will see how the UI (which is under a different namespace) talks to BL without even knowing about DAL.

Layer 3: The UI Layer

Here is the code in the `AllCustomers.aspx.cs` page that shows a list of all of the customers from the DB (there is a data list on the web form, which will show a list of the customers):

```
using DomainModel.BL;
namespace DomainModel.UI
    {
    //page load
    private void FillAllCustomers()
        {
            Customer c = new Customer();
            c.GetAll();
            List<Customer> cuList = c.CustomerCollection;
            dtlstAllCustomer.DataSource = cuList;
            dtlstAllCustomer.DataBind();
        }
    }
```

So in the UI class, we neither have any data access code (as we had in the previous chapter), nor are we calling data access class methods from this layer (as was the case with the 1-tier 2-layer style we saw earlier in this chapter). We have a reference to the BL layer (using `DomainModel.BL`), and we are using the Customer business object to return a generic list of customer objects, which we are binding to the data list control (showing a list of all the customers). So the GUI layer does not know anything about the DAL layer, and is completely independent of it.

The idea here is to understand how a 3-Layer architecture can provide more flexibility and loose-coupling to your project. In the next section, we will learn how we can use object data source controls to implement a 3-layer architecture without writing much code ourselves.

Object Data Source Controls

We looked at the data source controls in the last chapter and saw how they replaced the data access code, but tightly coupled the GUI to the data methods. To overcome this problem, Microsoft introduced object data source controls, so that we can bind directly to business objects, making it possible to use them in a 3-tier architecture.

Let's see how using object data source controls will shape our application:

1. Create a new web project using VS.

2. Add a new form named `datasource-customer.aspx`.

3. Add an object data source control, as shown here (drag and drop the object data source control from the **Data** tab under **ToolBox** in VS):

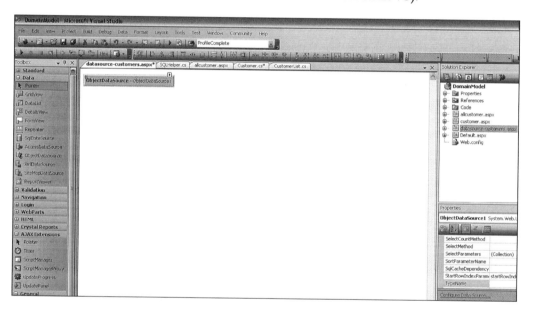

4. Now, we need to configure this object data source control. We first need to set the **Business object** , where we select our customer class:

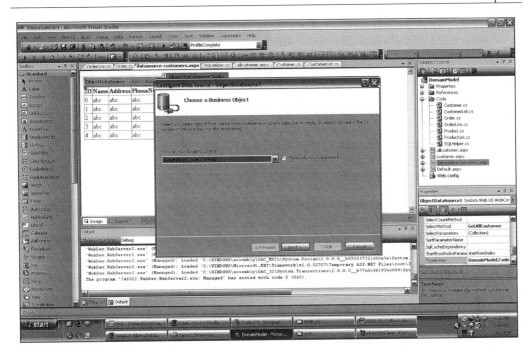

5. Then, we need to set the **SELECT**, **UPDATE**, and **INSERT** methods. For our sample, we will just set the **SELECT** method:

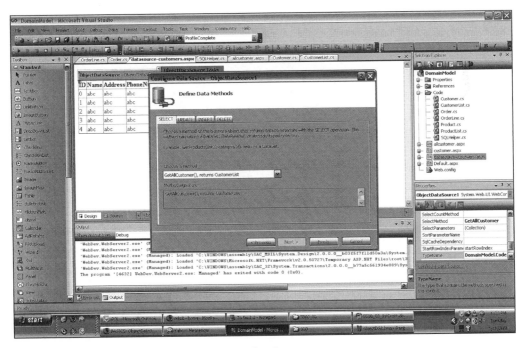

6. Then, we select **Finish**. We then add a **GridView** control on the same page and set the data source to our object data source control:

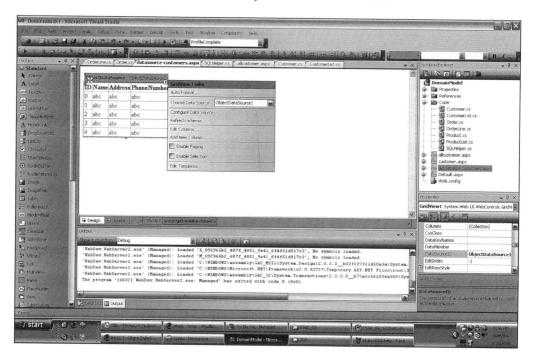

7. Now we run the page, and voila! We see all of the records without using any code in the UI layer!

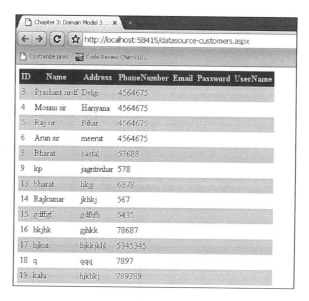

As we can see, using object data source controls complements the domain model and helps us avoid writing the UI layer code, as we can directly bind custom entities to data-bound controls in UI.

However, there are a few issues in using object data source controls:

- They are not very flexible. Sometimes we need to display data in UI in a complex way (which can be user friendly, but code un-friendly). In such cases, it is best to use and manipulate custom collections using manual coding; you cannot even extend the control to customize it.

- There is a slight performance hit when using object data source controls instead of using manual coding. This hit comes through the use of reflection by the control to access a class's attributes and methods.

 Reflection is a technique which VS uses to get metadata information about other entities, such as a class file or an assembly. Using reflection, the object data source control will first "read" the class to get all of the attributes and then use this metadata to connect to and perform operations on the class. On account of this additional "reading" step, the application suffers a performance hit.

Therefore, for a flexible approach, it is best to use custom code. But for small projects where we don't foresee any major complexity and performance issues, object data source controls are a good option to save on development time while supporting a flexible n-layer option.

Summary

All of the samples we covered in this chapter were of the 1-tier n-layer style. We learned how to create a 1-tier 2 layer architecture using logical code separation. Then we focused on the need for a 3-layered solution and examined ER-diagrams, domain models and UML, all of which are important tools that aid in the understanding of commercial projects required to build a 3-layered structure.

Then we focused on a 3-layered application structure for OMS, and looked at how both custom code and object data source controls can be used in this architecture.

In the coming chapters, we will discuss the need to physically separate this 3-layered code into "tiers", and see how we need a different model to achieve this goal and create scalable n-tier applications.

4
N-Tier Architecture

In the previous chapters we have seen, through code samples, how 1-tier 2-layer and 1-tier 3-layer solutions work in our ASP.NET web projects, and the advantages of going for a 3-layered architecture to create scalable and maintainable web applications. In all of the high-level architectural configurations we have studied up to now, we were dealing with the basic structuring and coding of the main ASP.NET application code—the Visual Studio solution, to be more precise. We had not considered the database and the client browser as separate physical tiers. We did this because we wanted to focus on how we can structure our main application solution in terms of layers and tiers. However, from this chapter onwards, we will include the physical database and the browser as distinct tiers being a part of the whole application. The reason for this change is because from now on we will be breaking our 1-tier application into multiple physical tiers (and not simply layers) and see how the entire distributed system works in collaboration. The term *distributed system* involves:

- The main ASP.NET application code, which will be broken down further into separate physical tiers so that each tier or assembly can be used independently of the others

- The physical database (an external RDMBS such as MS SQL Server, or any external storage such as XML files), also called the Data Tier

- The client browser (Internet Explorer or Firefox where the HTML will be rendered) also called the Presentation Tier

In this chapter we will learn:

- Why we need N-tier based systems
- How to create a 4-tier architecture
- How to create a 5-tier architecture
- What Data Transfer Objects are
- What a Lazy Loading design pattern is

Here, we will move from the basic 3-tier client-server model described in the previous chapters, to a four, five, or higher tiered architectures—in short, n-tier systems. Before moving ahead, let me emphasize an important point: it is very crucial to understand that there is no perfect architecture. Each application is unique, and therefore there can be different ways to implement an n-tier architecture. Hence, we will learn and understand the basic fundamentals of the n-tier system, and implement it in one particular style. The concepts discussed in this chapter will be generic enough to help you learn and apply your own customized n-tier style suited to the unique need of each project.

Why N-Tier?

"**N-tier**" is a team that almost every software developer knows, and a team that has been hugely debated across forums, blogs and offline discussion groups. During my early years as a programmer, I was so impressed with n-tier architecture that I thought every application should be n-tier, without even understanding the high-level view, which I eventually realized comes later with experience! To n-tier or not is the question for which we will try to find an answer in this chapter.

We have already seen 1-tier architectures, and if we keep the database on a separate machine with its own CPU, we will have a rudimentary 3-tier architecture in our web projects, as shown here:

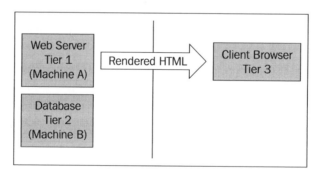

We have already seen how to break the main application tier in the above 3-tier application into logical layers. Now, the first question that comes to one's mind is why, exactly, do we need to break these logical layers into their own, separate, physical assemblies as tiers.

The answer is that **n-tiered development** allows a component-based approach to software design, allowing developers to make updates and changes to individual tiers without breaking other code. Let me explain this further.

When we talk about n-tier applications, we are referring to medium-size to enterprise-size applications. Many beginner developers have this urge to make every software system they develop an n-tier system, even when the project doesn't need to be tiered at all. For example, it would not be worth developing a simple guestbook application for a personal website on an n-tier architecture as it would take a lot of time and money, besides complicating the simple system for no tangible benefits.

But we need to think beyond layers and 1-tier applications when we deal with applications such as commercial websites with large user bases, medium to large software systems that need built-in interoperability and redundancy, and flexibly-distributed solutions. We need to separate out the business logic and data access code into their own assemblies to make the application further distributed and loosely-coupled in nature.

The parameters described in the following sections can be used to decide whether we want to go for a n-tier system or a simple layered solution.

Performance

Application performance is always a prime consideration when working on any project. The more the code is separated into different assemblies, the slower it becomes. See this diagram here:

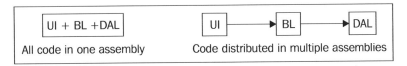

The reason for this slow performance is simple. It takes longer for a method in one assembly to call a method in another assembly than it would take if the method was in the same assembly. Some time is needed to refer to the other assembly, and read, find, and execute the required code. This time can be avoided if we have the code in the same physical DLL.

So if we separate the logically-layered code into different physical assemblies, then we will suffer a mild performance hit. I used the word **mild** because modern machines have a lot of computing power, and the performance hit is almost negligible. So if we consider this mild performance hit, then how can an architecture based on n-tier actually increase performance of the application?

It all depends on the way a single-processor on a machine works. On a single-processor machine, all operations, including the code executing the UI and the business logic, the connection to the database server (which is another application), fetching data, and so on, are handled by a single CPU. So it can handle only one instruction at a time. If the application has a long list of pending operations, then the processor will be hogged and will run slow, causing a bottleneck. But if we can distribute the application load so that we can use multiple processors (on multiple machines), then we can have substantial performance gains. Of course, to reap this benefit, the load itself should be quite high in the first place. If the load is always low, then we will lose more from having distributed tiers "talk" to each other than we will gain from distributing the workload.

So should we put the DAL and BL assemblies on different machines to balance load? The answer is no. The reason being the fact that before deciding to allocate the tiers to their own processors (by putting them on different machines with own CPU), we first need to identify the main load bearing components.

Before we go further, we need to understand the term "load". In web applications, load refers to the quantum of computing power required to serve client requests. In most web based applications, the load is usually handled by:

- A database
- The ASP.NET worker process (`w3wp.exe` in Windows 2003/2008, or `aspnet_wp.exe` in Windows XP)

For large load applications, it is advisable to have the database on a separate, dedicated machine, so that it does not compete with the ASP.NET worker process for CPU cycles. Here is the configuration:

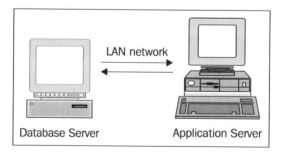

Database Server   Application Server

 ASP.NET worker process is an OS-level process which handles the .NET runtime. IIS handles the client requests and passes them on to the ASP.NET worker process.

In the previous diagram, the database is now on a different machine and is communicating with the application server (where the ASP.NET worker process runs) across high-speed Local Area Network (LAN). There would be a little latency involved here because data has to go through the LAN to reach the database, but that would be negligible because the LAN would usually be based on a fiber optics network and would be super-fast as both systems are on a local network. But we would gain considerable performance benefits because the database tier now has its own dedicated processor and memory.

Now, the UI, BL and DAL DLLs execute under the ASP.NET worker process application domain. So they share the same application domain and hence form a single component handling the server load. If we put the BL and DAL assemblies on separate machines then we will suffer a big performance hit, because the assemblies individually don't handle much load. Moreover, a lot of CPU cycles would be wasted in serializing data across cross-application boundaries.

> **Serialization** is the process of converting an object to some persistent medium so that we can transfer it across the network. For example, consider a Customer class object in our OMS application. Say we want to send this object to another computer across the network where another .NET application is expecting it. This object right now is in memory, so we can convert it into an XML string (serialize it) and then transfer this XML string to another machine over the network, where the .NET runtime will catch this XML string and convert it back to an object in memory (de-serialization).

This is how the configuration will look if we put the BL and DAL tiers on different machines:

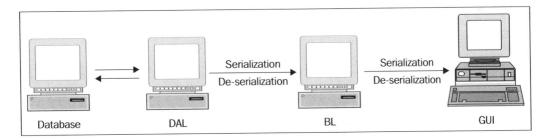

This serialization process is CPU intensive, and would hurt the performance more because it is actually not reducing any load but adding to it. The reason is that the BL or DAL alone does not handle the load individually. DAL is simply a utility layer that talks to the database and gets data from or sends data to BL. BL processes it and passes it on the GUI. In most systems, it is best to keep these three under the same application domain (worker process) so that we can do away with serialization overheads. There are cases where we might want to put some application components on a different server, for example, imagine a catalog management website with a large number of users. The search catalog part of this website would be heavily used and can be treated as a load-bearing component. In this case, it can be advantageous to move the search into its own machine, and return the results to the application tier using XML, or binary serialization, or similar methods.

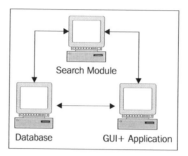

As shown in this diagram, we have placed another load bearing component on a separate machine to increase the overall performance of the web application. But if the application is small or does not get many hits, then cross-application serialization will hurt performance, and using such a configuration will be worthless.

These configurations are not possible without an n-tier architecture. But one must know when to use an n-tier architecture and when to go for a much simpler architectural configuration, depending on the actual project needs. There must be a balance between performance and application complexity.

Scalability

Application scalability is another important architectural aspect. Being scalable means being able to handle an increased load in future. For example, a community-based web application architecture should be capable of supporting an increased number of simultaneous users over time. If the number of concurrent users grows rapidly, then it's better to separate the components of your application onto different servers because CPU bandwidth is limited (as explained in the performance section). Components here not only mean the business logic and the data access code, but also accessing other static resources such as images, videos, and so on.

Scalability is closely tied to performance. Sometimes, for small applications such as a guestbook, we design a 1-tier 1-layer architecture, which is good performance-wise, but will not be scalable. We don't need scalability in such small applications as there is no requirement for it. But for bigger applications, a 1-tier configuration will not work, and we will need to break it into an n-tier based architecture so that the application becomes scalable and also more performance-efficient during peak load times.

Re-usability

If application code can be re-used within itself, or for some other external application, then not only do we save development and maintenance costs, but we also avoid code replication and make our code componented. For example, assume that you are developing an **Order Management System (OMS)** for a company. Now the company wants to re-use the business logic and data access code in their own small applications that might not be a part of the OMS you are developing. If you do not separate your code into separate physical assemblies, they won't be able to re-use your code easily. It would be too cumbersome to make a copy of your code as it is and then use it in a third-party application. Sometimes, it is not even possible to make this copy, like the other system is using a different .NET language than the one used by your OMS. So a physical separation is inevitable in such scenarios. Once this is done, we can give them individual assemblies, such as a data access code wrapped inside a DLL, so that they don't have to write DAL of their own and can use our assembly instead. This method of programming is called developing an **Application Programming Interface (API)**. It is an important principle in software programming to remove rigidity and make your application components re-usable in other applications.

> Application Programming Interface, or API development, is considered a very important principle in software design and development. Each method you write in code, if written properly, can be considered an API. The more loosely-coupled and flexible your code is, the more API-like it becomes. This helps you distribute your code and make it re-usable.

Loose-Coupling

If the code you write in one layer is highly-dependent on the code in some other layer, then your code is tightly-coupled, which means changing any part of it might break the other parts on which it is dependent. For example, in a 1-tier 2-layer system that we studied in Chapter 3, the UI code was calling the data access layer from the code-behind classes. This means that if the data access method has any error, the UI code will break. So UI and DAL are tightly-coupled. In the same chapter, we learnt the 3-layer model, where the UI interacted with business logic (BL) classes, which in turn called DAL methods. So if the DAL method breaks, the UI may not break as easily as in the first case, because we have made the layers loosely-coupled by bringing in a third layer (BL).

If we can make the higher-level components of our application independent of each other, then our application will become loosely-coupled. This means that changing one of the layers or tiers should not break the other layers. For example, if your DAL code is not properly abstracted but is tightly wound with the other layers above or below it, then it would be difficult to re-use it in any other application. So if someone makes a mistake in the DAL, the entire application will break down.

To avoid rigidity in large software systems, the concept of "implementation of loose coupling" is very important. N-tier architecture makes it possible to bring in loose coupling into our applications.

Plug and Play

To understand the Plug and Play functionality, consider the OMS example given earlier. Consider the requirement of making the application database agnostic. This means that the same application should work with MS SQL Server as well as with Oracle or any other database. So we need to make our DAL code capable of switching between databases. To achieve this, we create different DAL assemblies each having the code targeted to each database type, and we load a specific DAL assembly at runtime based on a key value in a `config` file. This means that our application is Plug and Play.

Another simple example can be a file encryption program that needs to support multiple encryption algorithms. The user should be able to select a particular algorithm from among all of the choices for encrypting files. These are two simple examples of where a Plug and Play type architecture would be required. The application would be developed from ground up to be able to support a Plug and Play based style. Also, this would give the developer the opportunity to write code to support other databases or algorithms later on without changing any code in the main application. A well-known design pattern that can be used in such cases is known as **Dependency Injection** (**DI**, which we will learn in the coming chapters).

All of the above points are major reasons to consider an n-tier architecture and make applications more scalable, robust, and loosely-coupled. In the coming sections, we will learn how to break layers into physical tiers and implement an n-tier architecture in our Order Management System, addressing what possible options we have, and which ones to select depending on the project needs.

A 4-Tier Approach

In the last chapter, we saw how layers nicely separated the application code into logical partitions. Now Breaking them further into separate physical assemblies will introduce some slight complexity, and to handle that we need to follow some design patterns.

At the simplest level, this is how we can segregate the application to have the following four tiers:

- Presentation tier: client-side browser
- UI tier: Web project having ASPX/ASCX, code-behind files
- Data access and business logic tier: in a separate class library project
- Data tier: the physical database

Note that in our first step to moving from a standard 3-tier web based application to 4-tier architecture, we are separating the DAL and BL code from the main web application into its own assembly. In a later section of this chapter, we will see how we can separate the DAL and BL into different assemblies.

To separate the BL and DAL code from logical layers (in the last chapter) to physical assemblies, we first need to follow these simple steps:

1. Create a new ASP.NET Web project in Visual Studio 2008 and name it **OMS.WebTier**.

2. Create a new class library project named **OMS.CodeTier** that will hold the business logic as well as data access files.

3. Move all of the files from the BL and DAL folders we used in the old GUI project (from Chapter 3) into this new class library project. We just need to modify the namespaces used (we will see the code to do this soon).

4. Add a reference to this class library project in the main web project.

Here is the solution structure image (in Visual Studio):

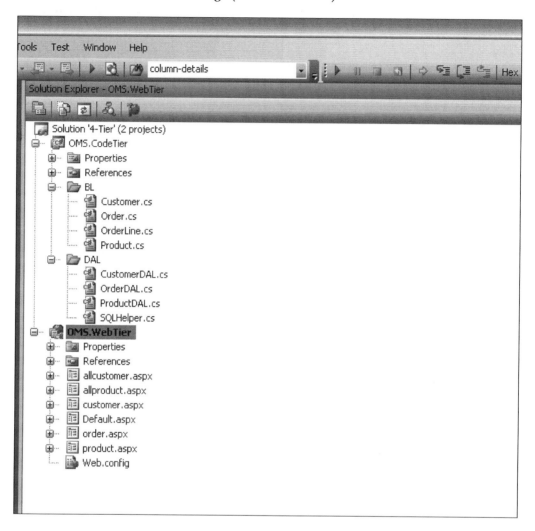

In the above solution structure, we have a GUI tier (**OMS.WebTier**), which will have all of the web pages, user controls and code-behind classes. This GUI tier will have a reference to a class library project named **OMS.CodeTier**, which will have the complete business logic and data access code separated into different folders under different namespaces. So from the 1-tier approach in the previous chapters, we now have a 2-tier solution, and along with having presentation and the database as separate tiers, we have implemented a classic 4-tier application architecture for our Order Management System. Now let us study how the coding looks for this 4-tier sample. Most of the code is similar to the code in Chapter 3.

Here is the code for the Customer class:

```
using OMS.CodeTier.DAL;
namespace OMS.CodeTier.BL
{
    public class Customer
    {

        private int _ID;
        private string _name;
        private string _address;
        //more private members go here
        public int ID
        {
            get { return _ID; }
            set { _ID = value; }
        }
        public string Name
        {
            get { return _name; }
            set { _name = value; }
        }
        //more properties go here
        public void Add()
        {
            CustomerDAL.AddCustomer(this);
        }
        public void Delete(int customerID)
        {
            CustomerDAL.DeleteCustomer(this.ID);
        }
        //other methods..
    }
}
```

We have already seen all of these methods in Chapter 3. The only difference in this chapter is that instead of being in a logical layer inside the main web project, the BL classes are physically separated into another tier, and will compile into a different assembly.

The same thing goes for the DAL code. It is exactly the same as in Chapter 3, but is now under a different project and a new assembly.

Note that the BL code and the DAL code are still not physically separated. They are logically partitioned under different namespaces but under the same assembly (which means that they are under the same tier). But the GUI tier is now different from the BL and DAL tiers. This gives us the flexibility to change the BL and DAL assembly without re-compiling the GUI tier. Also, this structure gives us the flexibility to use the current **OMS.CodeTier** assembly in other GUIs in addition to this one. For example, we can refer to and add this assembly to a Windows-based console application for our Order Management System, making our code more re-usable.

So we have achieved a greater degree of loose-coupling than the 1-tier solution architecture we studied in the previous chapters. In the next section, we will further de-couple the BL and DAL into separate tiers, and understand the 5-tier architectural approach.

5-Tier Architecture

With a 5-tier system, we introduce more redundancy into the application as a whole, along with separating the BL and DAL code into physical assemblies. This is how a sample 5-tier system would look like:

- Presentation tier
- UI tier
- Logical tier containing business logic (BL tier)
- Data access tier (DAL tier)
- Data tier (physical database)

Now why do we need to separate the logical layer and data layer into physical tiers? There can be many reasons to go for this architectural configuration. Some of them are listed here:

- You want further decoupling of the layers to introduce a flexible architecture for your project. Let me explain this further. When we have business and data access code in the same assembly (but logically separated in different files or using namespaces), we cannot distribute the code separately. In most enterprise applications, there is a greater need for code re-use. Some third-party applications might want to use our applications' business logic code (such as consuming an API) and some might want to use our data access code. In such cases, if we go for a layered solution, then changing anything in DAL would necessitate re-compiling the whole assembly, which also includes business logic assembly too. And this unnecessary change might create ripple effects in the application as the same DLL might be used in other third-party applications. So this should be avoided for large enterprise applications. For flexible adaptability, it is better to separate BL and DAL into their own assemblies.

- We might want to target different physical databases instead of one single database. For example, our application might need to support MS SQL Server, Oracle and MySQL. For this to happen, we need to keep the DAL code completely out of and independent from BL so that we can easily implement a Plug and Play based architecture.

- We might want to sell individual components separately. For example, some clients might want only the DAL assembly for use in their enterprise, while some others might want both the BL and DAL assemblies, and create a custom UI. Keeping components physically separate might be financially beneficial for large commercial applications.

> Note that the more we break our application into assemblies, the more performance hit we incur. However, as machine power quickly advances, a performance hit is a negligible price to pay for the overall gain in scalability as well as flexibility.

So it is beneficial to have a 5-tier architecture for relatively-large commercial applications, as this will promote better code maintenance, re-use, scalability, and adaptability.

Data Transfer Objects

The following diagram shows us how the 5-tier architecture would look like in our web applications:

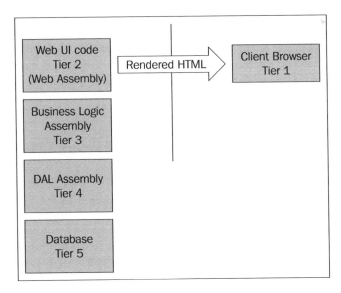

In this diagram, as UI, BL, and DAL are all in different tiers, we will need to add a reference to the project that is consuming another different project (say a GUI consuming a business class library project). But this brings us to a new problem—how to communicate effectively between any two tiers. Let me explain this in detail.

When the BL and DAL tiers were together in the same layer, we had no external dependencies, and we could easily call and refer to the objects of other classes by including the relevant namespaces. But now, the DAL tier will need to refer to a BL layer object in order to fill them or interact with them. But the BL tier also needs to refer the DAL tier so that BL methods can call DAL methods. This brings us to a cyclical reference issue. Refer the following diagram:

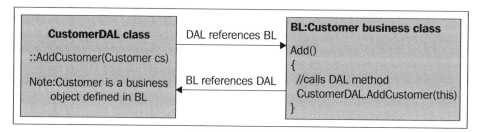

From this diagram, we can see that a need arises for both the BL and DAL to refer to each other because both are now separate projects, and also how this will lead to a cyclic reference issue, causing the compiler to immediately generate an error!

So we need to add a level of indirection to avoid this cyclical reference. There are many ways to achieve this, but one good, easy, and flexible method is to use **Data Transfer Objects**, or **DTOs**.

DTOs are simple objects with no defined methods, and having only public members. They are like carriers of data to and from the layers. Some people use strongly typed datasets for the same purpose.

The reason why we need DTOs is because passing business objects through layers is cumbersome as business objects are quite "heavy" and carry a lot of extra information with them, which is usually not needed outside the layers. So instead of passing business objects we create lightweight DTOs and make them serializable.

Let's understand how to use DTOs, through an example. We will create a 5-Tier solution for our Order Management System. Create a new VS solution, and add projects as shown here:

- 5Tier.DAL: This class library project will encapsulate all of the data access logic. This DAL layer will **not** reference BL layer, but will communicate with it using DTOs defined in the common layer. So this DAL project references only the 5Tier.Common project.

- 5Tier.Common: This class library project will have code that is common to all layers (such as enumerated types) and will also hold Data Transfer Objects. This project will be referenced by all layers, since it is common to all of them.

- 5Tier.Business: This class library project will handle all business objects and will call the DAL project and pass data to and from it using DTOs. So this project will reference the 5Tier.Common project as well as the NTier.DAL project.

- 5Tier.Web: This web project will have the UI layer and will also use DTOs to display and pass data. It will reference the 5Tier.Common and 5Tier.Business projects only.

The following diagram shows how these tiers would interact with each other:

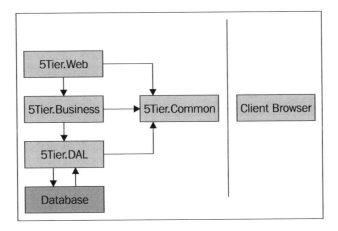

 Some of you might be thinking why I did not call this system a 6-tier system. Since we have the 5Tier.Common project compiling to a separate physical assembly, we can include it as another tier and refer the system as one belonging to 6-tier architecture instead of a 5-tier one. But as I said earlier, there are no strict rules and it is up to us to define and configure the application.

I do not see the Common project as a separate tier as I treat the DTOs as *transient structures*, which pass through the different tiers and can be accessed by any layer. So I do not treat them as a separate tier. But if you do want to name it separately, there is nothing wrong with that convention either.

Let us start with the code in the business layer. Here, I will highlight the important portions of the code to understand the architectural aspects of this 5-tier configuration.

Take the example of what the `Customer` class will look like in this business tier. This class will be similar to the 4-tier business classes we saw earlier, and will have all of the same attributes as well as methods such as `Add()`, `Update()`, `Delete()`, `Find()`. Now, instead of putting all fields as private variables and then making properties inside the `Customer` class, we first create a DTO named `CustomerDTO` in the Common project encapsulating all the customer-related attributes.

Create two new class library projects as follows:

- `5Tier.Business`
- `5Tier.Common`

In the 5Tier.Common project, create a new folder named DTO. Add a new class file named `CustomerDTO`, which has the following code:

```
using System;
using System.Collections.Generic;

namespace 5Tier.Common
{
   /// <summary>
   ///DTO for the 'Customer' object.
   /// </summary>
   [Serializable]
   public class CustomerDTO
   {
       #region Constructors
        ///<summary>
       /// Default constructor
           ///</summary>
        public CustomerDTO()
       {
          this.loadStatus = LoadStatus.Initialized;
       }

       ///<summary>
       /// Copy constructor
       ///</summary>
        public CustomerDTO(CustomerDTO sourceDTO)
       {
           loadStatus = dto.LoadStatus;
           ID = sourceDTO.ID;
           Name = sourceDTO.Name;
           Address = sourceDTO.Address;
           PhoneNo = sourceDTO.PhoneNo;
```

```
          UserName = sourceDTO.UserName;
          Password = sourceDTO.Password;
          Email = sourceDTO.Email;
       }
       #endregion

       public  LoadStatus              loadStatus;

       public System.Int32 ID;
       public System.String  Name = null;
       public System.String  Address = null;
       public System.String  PhoneNo = null;
       public System.String  UserName = null;
       public System.String  Password = null;
       public System.String  Email = null;


    }//end class
  }//end namespace
```

Let us understand this code, step-by-step. First note that each DTO class would be marked with an attribute (`Serializable`). This is because the DTOs would be transferred across the tiers, and as explained earlier in this chapter, we need to serialize data so that it can be transferred and deserialized by other applications. In our sample, if we have the `5Tier.Common` assembly running in the same process as the `5Tier.Business` and `5.GUI`, then this serialization process will not be necessary as there would be no cross-application domain call. But there can be cases when either the BL, the DAL or the GUI assemblies can be separated physically and located on a different tier. In these cases, there would be cross-boundary and cross-application domain communication. We will need to serialize all of the DTOs so that they can pass through the network across application domains. The `Serializable` attribute marks the class as serializable so that .NET runtime can handle this serialization work for us. You can get better control over the entire serialization/deserialization process by using custom serialization, where you need to write the code manually.

Next, in the `CustomerDTO` class, we have defined all of the attributes as public variables and set them to their default values. We should try to use only primitive data types in DTOs as they should be kept as simple as possible. If they are not generic enough, we can have problems in using them in remote calls by different language libraries (as they might not have those specific data types defined).

We have also defined a `copy constructor` in our DTO class, which just copies the data from another DTO to populate the attributes in the current DTO. We will see the importance of this when creating business layer classes.

Lazy Loading

An important thing to note here is a variable named `LoadStatus`. This is used to implement lazy loading, a design pattern that helps us make our application more efficient by loading only the required data. Using lazy loading pattern, we can defer the loading of all of the properties of an object until they are really needed. Let me explain with an example. In our OMS application, consider a form that shows the list of all of the customers in a grid. Now, in this form, only the `Customer ID`, the `first name` and the `last name` are shown, along with an `edit` and `delete` button. The `Customer address`, `email address`, `password` and other fields are shown only when someone edits an existing customer or adds a new one, a process which is done through another form. So if we want to load a list of `Customer` objects on this `Customer List` form, we don't need to fetch all the fields at once from the database. We only need to fetch the `Customer ID`, `first name` and `last name` fields to make our application more performance-efficient (by getting only the data required). And when we are on the `Edit Customer` form, we need to fetch all of the details. This can be done by having two methods in the DAL: one for a partial fetch and another for a complete fetch. But this approach is cumbersome, and we cannot always write two methods for each entity like this. So we follow the lazy loading design pattern, and use an enum named `LoadStatus` in our code, which can have one of three status values:

- `Initialized`
- `Ghost load`: object is partially loaded
- `Loaded`: object is completely loaded

We will see in the business and data access classes how we are using the lazy loading design to make our application more efficient.

Coming back to our DTO class, note that we have used the status value of `Initialized` in our default constructor when creating a new DTO. This indicates that the state of the DTO is initialized and there is no actual data in it, only default values. Also, as you might have noticed, we have not added any method here because the DTO is simply a data carrier, and not a business object in any sense.

Now we create the business class, `Customer.cs`, in the Business Tier
(`5Tier.Business` project):

```
using NTier.Common;
using NTier.DAL;
namespace NTier.BAL
{
    /// <summary>
    ///  Business class for the 'Customer'.
    /// </summary>
    public class Customer
{
        private CustomerDTO _customerDTO;

        #region Default Constructor
        /// <summary>
        /// Default Constructor initializes
        /// a new DTO object so that the business
        /// object is ready to be used.
        /// </summary>
        public Customer()
        {
          _customerDTO = new CustomerDTO();
        }

        #endregion

        #region Copy Constructor
        /// <summary>
        /// Copy Constructor initializes new business
        /// object by copying exisitng DTO to a
        /// a new DTO object
        /// </summary>
        public Customer(CustomerDTO _sourceDTO)
        {
          _customerDTO = new CustomerDTO(_sourceDTO);
        }
        #endregion

        #endregion

        #region Public Properties

        public CustomerDTO DTO
```

```
{
   get { return _customerDTO ; };
   set { _customerDTO = value ;};
}

public System.Int32 ID
{
   get { return _customerDTO.ID; }
   set { _customerDTO.ID = value; }
}

public System.String  Name
{
    get
     {
      Load();
        return  _customerDTO.Name;
     }
    set { _customerDTO.Name  = value;}
}

public System.String  Address
{
    get
     {
      Load();
        return  _customerDTO.Address;
     }
    set { _customerDTO.Address  = value;}
}

public System.String  PhoneNo
{
    get
     {
      Load();
        return  _customerDTO.PhoneNo;
     }
    set { _customerDTO.PhoneNo  = value;}
}

public System.String  UserName
{
    get
```

```
      {
       Load();
         return   _customerDTO.UserName;
      }
      set {  _customerDTO.UserName   = value;}
   }

public System.String   Password
{
     get
       {
        Load();
          return   _customerDTO.Password;
       }
     set {  _customerDTO.Password   = value;}
  }

public System.String   Email
{
     get
       {
        Load();
          return   _customerDTO.Email;
       }
     set {  _customerDTO.Email   = value;}
  }

#endregion Public Properties

#region Private Methods
/// <summary>
/// Helper function used in lazy load; if the load state
/// is "Ghost" (partial loaded) then do a full load
/// </summary>
private void Load()
{
   try
     {
        if( _customerDTO.loadStatus == LoadStatus.Ghost)
        {
          _customerDTO=CustomerDAL.LoadCustomer( _customerDTO.ID);
          _customerDTO.loadStatus = LoadStatus.Loaded ;
```

```
            }
        }
    catch(Exception ex)
      {
          //log exception
          throw;
      }
}

#endregion Private Methods

#region   Public Methods

#region Update
/// <summary>
/// Updates object state into database
/// </summary>
/// <returns>bool</returns>
public bool Update()
{
    try
    {
       ///<remark>
       ///Check for the load status to make sure that update is
       ///not being called on disconnected/'ghost' loaded objects.
       ///</remark>
       if( _customerDTO.loadStatus == LoadStatus.Loaded)
       {
           CustomerDAL.UpdateCustomer(_customerDTO);

       ///<remarks>
           ///Set load status to 'ghost' to mark that it needs to
           ///be fully loaded again
           ///</remarks>
           _customerDTO.loadStatus=LoadStatus.Ghost;
           return true;
       }
       else
       {
           return false;
       }
       }
    catch(Exception ex)
    {
```

```
    //log error
        throw;
        }
    }
#endregion

#endregion Public Methods

}//end class
}//end namespace
```

Let us now analyze this business class. First of all we wrap the class attributes in the CustomerDTO class and aggregate it as a private member in this Customer business class as:

```
private CustomerDTO _customerDTO;
```

We then create class properties by using DTO fields in the get or set methods as:

```
public System.String  Password
    {
        get
        {
          Load();
            return  _customerDTO.Password;
        }
        set { _customerDTO.Password  = value;}
    }
```

In the get properties, note the Load() method being called. This is the implementation of the Lazy Loading design pattern. When the class object is first loaded from the database, we fill only the most needed properties such as ID, Name and so on. For all other properties, we load them on demand. This Load method in the properties will be called whenever the consumer of this business class tries to access that particular property value:

```
private void Load()
    {
        try
        {
            if( _customerDTO.loadStatus == LoadStatus.Ghost)
            {
              _customerDTO=CustomerDAL.LoadCustomer( _customerDTO.ID);
              _customerDTO.loadStatus = LoadStatus.Loaded ;
            }
        }


    }
```

Note that in this Load method above, we are first checking if the load status is Ghost (partially loaded) and if yes, then we are loading the customer DTO from the DAL and then changing the Load Status to Loaded (because now all of the properties would need to be loaded). This will make sure that we don't load the properties' values again when some other property value is accessed. In the DAL method, we check for the load status value, and then load partially or fully, based on the status value that is passed. Here is the code from the Customer DAL class (for clear understanding, I have removed the code unrelated to the current topic of discussion):

```
public static Collection<CustomerDTO> GetAllCustomers(LoadStatus
loadStatus …)
    {
    try
      {
    string strCommandText = "GetAllCustomers";
      Collection<CustomerDTO> list;
       using(SqlConnection cn = new SqlConnection(SQLHelper.
                                    GetConnectionString()))
       {
           SqlCommand cmd = new SqlCommand(strCommandText, cn);
           cmd.CommandType = CommandType.StoredProcedure;

    SqlDataReader reader = null;
    list = new Collection<CustomerDTO>();

    cn.Open();
     reader = cmd.ExecuteReader();
    if(reader.HasRows)
      {
        while(reader.Read())
        {
          //Create collection and fill
          CustomerDTO c = new CustomerDTO();

            c.ID = (System.Int32)reader["ID"];
            c.Name = reader["Name"];

          if(loadStatus==LoadStatus.Loaded)
          {
            c.Address = reader["Address"];
```

```
                  c.PhoneNo = reader["PhoneNo"];
                  c.UserName = reader["UserName"];
                  c.Password = reader["Password"];
                  c.Email = reader["Email"];
              }
              list.Add(c);
          }
          }
      }
      return list;
  }
```

In this DAL method, I am lazy loading all customers, which means that I check the load status (which is being passed as an argument), and then, if the status is loaded, I load fetch all properties from the database; otherwise I fetch only CustomerID and Name as these properties will be displayed in the front end, the CustomerList.aspx page. So we are not loading other properties that are not required on that particular page. But if we need to load them all at once, then we can pass in the Load Status value as Loaded to indicate to our DAL that it has to load all properties.

Performance note: Note the use of data readers for better performance. Data readers are read-only, one-way pointers to the database. Hence, they are much lighter and faster than data sets and data adapters (which in turn use data readers to map data). It is always better to use data readers for filling in custom entities so that we have a fine level of control over the data access process, in addition to gaining the performance advantage of a data reader.

Architectural note: Note that instead of returning List<Customer> we are returning Collection<Customer> from the DAL methods due to the fact that List<T> should be used for internal use only, not in public APIs. Now our DAL is made in an API-like fashion. To make sure that our API is extendable, we need to use Collection<T> as this is extendable, unlike List<T> where we cannot override any member. For example, we can override the SetItem protected method in Collection<T> to get notified when the collection is changed (such as adding a new item and so on). Besides this, List<T> has too much extra stuff that is useful for internal use only, and not as a return type to an API.

Updating Business Objects

Now let us see how we can update a `Customer` business object in the `Customer.cs` business class. Here is the code:

```
public bool Update()
    {
        try
        {
        ///<remark>
            ///Check for the load status to make sure that update is
            ///not being called on disconnected/'ghost' loaded objects.
            ///</remark>
            if( _customerDTO.loadStatus == LoadStatus.Loaded)
            {
                CustomerDAL.UpdateCustomer(_customerDTO);
                ///<remarks>
                ///Set load status to 'ghost' to mark that it needs to
                ///be fully loaded again
                 ///</remarks>
                _customerDTO.loadStatus=LoadStatus.Ghost;
                return true;
            }
            else
            {
                return false;
            }
        }
    }
```

In this `Update()` method, we first check if the `Customer` object to be updated is fully loaded or not, as there is no use performing an update action on a partially-loaded (or ghost loaded) `Customer` object (with only `Name` and `ID` fields). If the object is ghost loaded, we return the method `Call`, else we call the `Update` method of the DAL class to update the `Customer`.

After the DAL's `Update` method is called, we make sure that the `LoadStatus` of the `Customer` object is set to `Ghost`. This is done to make sure that all consumers of this object need to get the latest properties from the database, as it has been recently updated.

GUI Tier

Here is the front end code, which simply populates a repeater with all of the customer records:

```
<asp:Repeater ID="rptCustomers" runat="server"
        DataKeyField="CustomerID" >
<HeaderTemplate>

                        <tr>
                          <th>
                                ID
                          </th>
                          <th>
                                Name
                          </th>

                          <th>
                                Edit
                          </th>
                          <th>
                                Delete
                          </th>
                        </tr>

</HeaderTemplate>
 <ItemTemplate>

                    <tr>
                    <td>
                        <%#Eval("CustomerID")%>
                    </td>
                    <td>
                        <%#Eval("Name")%>
                    </td>

                    <td align="right">
                        <asp:Button ID="btnEdit" runat="server"
                            Text="Edit"
                            CommandArgument='
                            <%#Eval("ProductID")%>'
                            CommandName="edit"/>
                    </td>

                    <td align="right">
```

```
                         <asp:Button ID="btnDelete" runat="server"
                              Text="Delete"
                              CommandArgument='
                              <%#Eval("ProductID")%>'
                              CommandName="delete"/>
                    </td>

               </tr>

          </ItemTemplate>

     </asp:Repeater>
```

This is a simple repeater control which gets populated with a list of Customer objects from the database, using the following code in the CustomerList.aspx.cs file:

```
private void FillCustomers()
     {
          CustomerCollection list=new CustomerCollection();
          rptCustomers.DataSource = list.FindAll();
          rptCustomers.DataBind();
     }
```

The CustomerCollection class, which is defined in the next section, simply returns a collection of Customer objects. So the GUI tier is completely independent of the Data tier, and talks to the BL tier via a one-way reference (we have added a reference to the BL in the GUI tier, and not the other way round). So our system is loosely-coupled.

We can bind the Customer object properties in the ASPX using a declarative syntax, and if we need to edit a particular customer, we just need to directly use the *Customer* object's properties in the Editcustomer form, as in:

```
txtCustomerEmail.text = customer.Email;
```

When this property is called, the Load() method defined in the property will check if the Customer object is fully loaded or not; if not, it will load all of the properties. So this is called **load on demand** — the core principle of the lazy loading design pattern.

Generics and Custom Collections

In the above code samples, we saw the use of a lot of generics, which is a new feature starting from ASP.NET 2.0 onwards. Prior to .NET 2.0, developers used to write collection classes to hold a collection of objects. So a `Product` class would hold all of the product attributes plus the methods that perform operations on a single product such as `Update()` whereas the collection class contained methods such as `Find()`, `GetAllProducts()`, and so on.

With the introduction of generics, we can easily do away with custom collection classes. If the collection class has only standard functionality such as `Add`, `Remove()`, `GetXX()` and so on, then we can simply use generics for that. For example, the `Customer.cs` business class can have a collection object inside it say:

```
public class Customer
{
    private List<Customer> _customercollection;

}
```

So we can directly use generics instead of creating `custom` collection classes. But `custom collection` classes might be needed if we:

- Want a custom implementation of the generic `List<T>` method
- Need extra functionality, which the generic `List<T>` class doesn't offer

In these cases, we need to create our own collection class, which is basically a wrapper around the generic `List<T>` and add our own custom functions. If you look at the `Customer.cs` code or OMS code samples, you will notice that every business object (such as `Customer`) has only the following methods defined in the class:

- `Load`
- `Update`

Other methods such as `Add`, `Delete`, `FindAll`, `GetXX` and so on are defined in a `custom collection` class, because these methods operate on a "list" of entities, hence they belong to a `collection class` rather than the main entity class (like `Customer.cs`). Here is the `CustomerCollection` class for OMS:

```
public class CustomerCollection : Collection<Customer>
    {

        public CustomerCollection(): base(new List<Customer>)
        {

        }
```

```csharp
    public bool Add(Customer c)
    {
        try
        {
            DAL.Add(c.DTO);
            c.DTO.loadStatus=LoadStatus.Ghost;

            return true;
        }
    }

    public bool Delete( Customer c)
    {
        try
        {
            DAL.Delete(c.ID);
            c.DTO.loadStatus=LoadStatus.Ghost;

            return true;
        }
    }

public Collection<Customer> FindAll(LoadStatus loadStatus)
    {
        try
        {
            /*
             * Get the list of DTOs returned from the DAL and
             * create a collection of business objects by passing
             * in DTOs in the domain object constructor
             */
            Collection<CustomerDTO> dtoList =
                    CustomerDAL.GetAllCustomersNoPaging(loadStatus);
            foreach (CustomerDTO dto in dtoList)
            {
                Customer customer = new Customer(dto);
                this.Add(customer);
            }
            return this;
        }
        catch (Exception ex)
        {
            //handle exception
            throw;
        }
    }
```

The above `CustomerCollection` class is derived from `Collection<Customer>` because we don't want to derive it from `List<>` for the reasons mentioned earlier. Now we are passing a `List<>` in the default constructor because we might need to call some useful methods in `List<T>` and that's why we are encapsulating `List<T>` like this, deriving our `Collection<T>` using the base constructor so that the `Customer Collection` can simply call the underlying `List<T>`'s find (or any other useful method) implementation, saving us from having to implement our own.

Summary

We have seen how a 5-tier architecture works. An important point to note is that there can be multiple ways of implementing a 5-tier architecture, and no architectural implementation can be a silver bullet for your own custom project. The aim of this chapter is to give you an idea of and an approach to how a 5-tier design can be implemented in your own projects. But this is by no means the only best method to do so. Many experienced developers implement their own custom n-tier solutions, which can be very different from what we have seen in this chapter. But the basic concepts from an architectural standpoint would be similar to what we have learnt in this chapter, giving us the knowledge to customize our own implementation for our specific project needs.

We also covered some crucial architectural aspects and design patterns, such as loose coupling, a lack of strong dependency on other layers, scalability, and so on. An n-tier implementation involves more work and longer code files, but this is a small price to pay for greater benefits such as scalability, maintainability and flexibility, which are important for big projects.

It's important to understand that we should not blindly use an n-tier architecture in every project. We need to think about and foresee a need for such distributed architecture and then plan accordingly. Using a 5-tier architecture for a simple guestbook application for a personal website would be overkill, in addition to wasting time and resources. But it is a must for a large-scale inventory management system that needs to interact with other external systems such as accounting packages. With proper use, n-tier architecture can help organizations scale up without re-writing the entire application, and can save valuable man hours of work in the long run, as well as provide a stable and robust application platform for future growth.

5
Model View Controller

These days, **Model View Controller (MVC)** is a buzzword in the ASP.NET community, thanks to the upcoming ASP.NET MVC framework that Microsoft is expected to launch soon (at the time of writing of this book, only Preview 5 was available). This chapter is dedicated to MVC design and the ASP.NET MVC framework.

In this chapter, we will learn about MVC design patterns, and how Microsoft has made our lives easier by creating the ASP.NET MVC framework for easier adoption of MVC patterns in our web applications. The following are some highlights of this chapter:

- Understanding the Page Controller pattern
- Understanding the need for the MVC design pattern
- Learning the basics of MVC design
- Understanding the Front Controller design pattern
- Understanding REST architecture
- Understanding the ASP.NET MVC framework
- Implementing the ASP.NET MVC framework in a sample application

Page Controller Pattern in ASP.NET

So far, all web pages we have created in our coding samples are based on the page controller pattern, which is the default architecture in the ASP.NET web forms. Let us understand page controller in detail.

In Chapter 2, we noticed that inline coding samples in ASP and ASP.NET had HTML and code scripts mixed together, creating a hard-to-maintain code base. Then we studied how code-behind classes "modularized" the architecture by separating the logic from the HTML. This code-behind architecture is a page controller based design, where by controller we mean the components that control the rendering of the HTML, which in the case of ASP.NET web forms are the code-behind classes.

Each page has a code-behind class, and the URL requested by the client is directly handled by individual pages. Any button or server control causing postbacks (such as a DropDownList control) is handled directly by the page code-behind class. So understanding the page life cycle is very important in a page controller based architecture. Here is a diagram that shows how a page controller pattern works in ASP.NET:

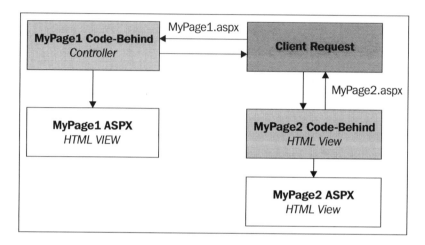

So for every page, its code-behind will act as a controller and handle all requests, and return processed HTML to the client browser.

Problems with Page Controller Design

In the page controller design we have a controller for each distinct page in our application (a separate code-behind class having all of the logic that fires sequentially as each page loads according to the ASP.NET page life cycle). So for big projects, there could potentially be a lot of code in the code-behind files, creating problems in code maintenance and support.

GUI Unit Testing

Separating business logic and data access code from the GUI is one of the steps leading towards a better design. In the previous chapters, we saw how to implement a basic n-tier architecture using tiers and layers to achieve loose coupling. But testing the application, especially the GUI and the code-behind classes in a page controller based model, is very difficult because the only way to test something like a button click's code-behind event handler is to click the button itself! This means that if we put more and more code in code-behind classes (which inevitably becomes the case in large web applications with lots of UI controls), we will not be able to run unit tests on the UI code. So the only way to test the application would be to manually test the GUI. The page controller based design does not support unit testing, and we would not be able to use automated unit testing tools such as NUnit, MBUnit and so on (which we can easily use to test the other layers such as BL and DAL).

There are ways to perform automated testing in GUI using testing tools that use Javascript to actually perform the button click events through the code, although they are clumsy and difficult to use. Even if we write scripts today, they will need to change if the GUI changes in the future, which is very much possible as the GUI can be changed many times during a project's lifetime and also after it is finished. This makes unit testing more difficult as one would need to rewrite the automated testing scripts on every GUI change. So most people tend to use brute force testing, which involves clicking all possible UI controls (such as buttons and so on) and verifying whether the code works as expected. This is a very time-consuming task, and if the GUI changes, the testing needs to be carried out again.

We will now see how MVC design helps us implement a clean separation between the UI and the controller, and also make our UI unit-testable.

MVC Design: A Front Controller based Approach

MVC, which stands for Model View Controller, is a design pattern that helps us achieve the decoupling of data access and business logic from the presentation code , and also gives us the opportunity to unit test the GUI effectively and neatly, without worrying about GUI changes at all. In this section, we will first study the basic MVC pattern and then move on to understanding the ASP.NET MVC framework.

A framework is a set of tools that includes libraries or methods developed according to a certain architecture, so that applications do not need to re-invent the wheel. Instead of re-writing the basic implementation each time, they can use the framework and abstract themselves from the internal framework implementation details.

Front Controller Design

MVC is based on a front controller design, where we have a centralized controller instead of multiple controllers, as was the case in the page controller based design that we saw earlier. By default, ASP.NET is page controller based. So making a front controller based project would require a lot of work (using HttpHandlers to route the requests manually). Basically, in a front controller design, we trap all of the client requests and direct them to a central controller, and the controller then decides which view to render (or which ASPX page to process). Here is how a basic model of a front controller design works:

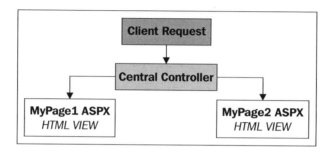

As you can see, the front controller sits at the "front" of all of the pages and renders a view based on logic in the central controller file. In the next section we will study and analyze exactly what goes on inside a controller, a view, and a model.

Basics of MVC

Let's first get into the theoretical aspects of MVC. MVC design has three major parts:

- **Model:** This refers to the data that is shown in the UI. This data can come from different sources, for example, a database.

- **View:** This refers to the user interface (UI) components that will show the model data.

- **Controller:** This controls when to change the view, based on user actions, such as button clicks.

In terms of ASP.NET web applications, the model, view, and controller participants can be identified as:

- **View:** This refers to HTML markup in ASPX pages, minus the code-behind logic. This view is rendered in the presentation tier (the browser).
- **Controller:** This refers to the special controller classes that decide which model needs to be shown to which particular view.
- **Model:** This refers to the data coming from the data layer, which may be processed by the business layer.

Before moving ahead, an important point to understand is that the MVC design is not a replacement to the n-tier architecture. MVC is more focused on how to keep the UI separate from the logic and the model; the model itself can be broken into separate tiers.

In the MVC design, the model, the view, and the controller are not related directly to the layers, or to the physical tiers; they are logical components that operate together in a certain pattern. The controller is related directly to the model and the view. Based on user actions (in the view), it fetches the data (the model) and populates the view. The relationship between the controller, the model, and the view can be depicted as:

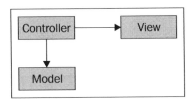

The view is based on the model, which means that its job is to simply render the model that the controller passes to it:

So the net relationship between the three components can be described as:

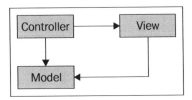

A few important points to note from the above diagram:

- We can see that the model depends neither on the view nor on the controller, which is logical. Think of it like this: we have some data in the database tables; we use DAL code to handle this data and BL code to operate on this data as per certain business rules. Now, it is up to the UI to present and show this data. But the data itself is not dependent on the graphical user interface (GUI). So the model is independent of the view and the controller.

- The view does not depend on the controller; rather, the controller is associated with the view. That means we have a separation between the view and the controller, allowing us to change views independent of the controller.

- The view depends on the model, and is updated when the model's state has changed. As the view cannot contain any logic (which is stored inside the model), the view depends on the model; that is, the model is in charge of updating the contents or displaying the view.

Now we will look at the practical aspects of implementing this MVC design using the ASP.NET MVC framework, which will help us implement our web applications. MVC will be ready in no time. But before going ahead with the actual code, we need to understand another important aspect of ASP.NET MVC framework, that is, REST!

REST: Representation State Transfer

REST means Representational State Transfer, an architectural pattern used to identify and fetch resources from networked systems such as the World Wide Web (WWW). The REST architecture was the foundation of World Wide Web. But the term itself came into being around the year 2000, and is quite a buzzword these days. The core principle of REST is to facilitate the sharing of resources via unique identifiers, just as we use Uniform Resource Identifiers (URIs) while accessing resources on the Web. In simple terms, REST specifies how resources should be addressed, including URI formats, and protocols such as HTTP. The term resources include files such as ASPX pages, HTML files, images, videos, and so on.

In the default page controller based design in ASP.NET, we don't follow a strict REST-based architecture. If we use a pure REST-based architecture, then all of the information required to access a particular resource would be in the URI. This means that we don't need to check if a postback happened or not, because each request is unique in itself and will be treated differently (via unique URLs). Whereas in ASP.NET, we can use the postback technique to make the same requests using the same URLs and do different processing based on whether it is a postback or not. Many a times, in numerous projects, we come across the following coding style in ASP.NET code-behind files:

```
btnSave_Cick()
{
    Response.Redirect("~/MyPage.aspx");
}
```

Here, on the postback (button click), we are redirecting the user to another resource (`mypage.aspx`), and this approach goes against the REST principle as we are delegating the responsibility to load a resource to another page based controller's postback event. This is not REST-like behavior. Now, we will see how MVC compliments the REST approach.

MVC and REST

MVC is radically different from the default page controller based design in the ASP.NET framework as it implements a front controller based design. In our normal applications, we use a lot of postbacks and make use of ViewState, and the development is centered around web forms. For each functional aspect, we may have a single webform; for example, for adding customers, we might create something like `AddCustomer.aspx`, and for showing a list of customers, we might use `CustomerList.aspx`.

But in an MVC architecture, webforms lose their importance. We don't create webforms in the same way that we do in standard ASP.NET applications. In the MVC framework, we use URL routing, which means that all URLs have some specific format, and the URLs are used based on the settings in a `config` file. In a standard ASP.NET application, the URL is linked to a specific ASPX file, say `http://localhost/CustomerList.aspx`. In MVC, the URL routes are defined in a REST-like fashion: `http://localhost/customer/list/`.

So in MVC, ASPX pages are reduced to simply showing the view; they will not have any code in their code-behind classes. What needs to be shown on an ASPX page will be handled by the Controller classes. ASPX will just be a kind of view engine and nothing else. ASPX will not have control-level event handlers or any kind of logic in the code-behind. In the next section, we will see how the ASP.NET MVC framework makes our life easier in adopting an MVC based approach in our projects.

ASP.NET MVC Framework

The ASP.NET MVC framework was released by Microsoft as an alternative approach to web forms when creating ASP.NET based web applications. The ASP.NET MVC framework is not a replacement or upgrade of web forms, but merely another way of programming your web applications so that we can get the benefits of an MVC design with much less effort.

As of now, the ASP.NET MVC framework is still in CTP (Community Technology Preview, which is similar to an advanced pre-stage), and there is no certain date when it will be released. But even with the CTP 5, we can see how it will help MVC applications follow a stricter architecture.

We will quickly see how to use the ASP.NET MVC framework through a small example.

Sample Project

First, download the ASP.NET MVC framework from the Microsoft website and install it. This installation will create an MVC project template in VS 2008.

Start VS 2008, select the **File | New Project** menu item and then choose the **ASP.NET MVC Web Application** template to create a new web application using this template.

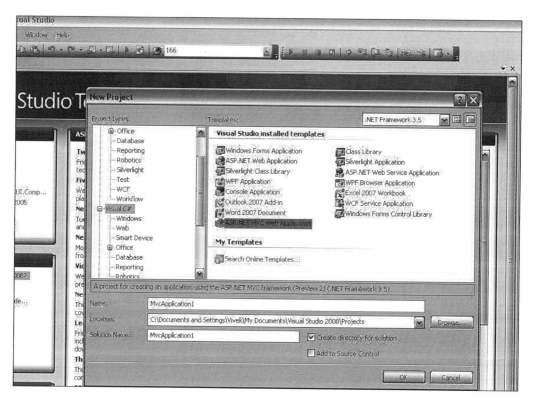

By default, when you create a new application using this option, Visual Studio will ask you if you want to create a Unit Test project for your solution, with a drop-down list pre-populated with the different possible types of test frameworks (the default would be VS test, but in case you installed MBUnit or NUnit, these would also be populated here):

There are many free unit testing frameworks available for ASP.NET projects, and NUnit and MBUnit are two of the most popular ones. Here are the links:

MBUnit: `http://www.mbunit.com/`

NUnit: `http://www.nunit.org/index.php`

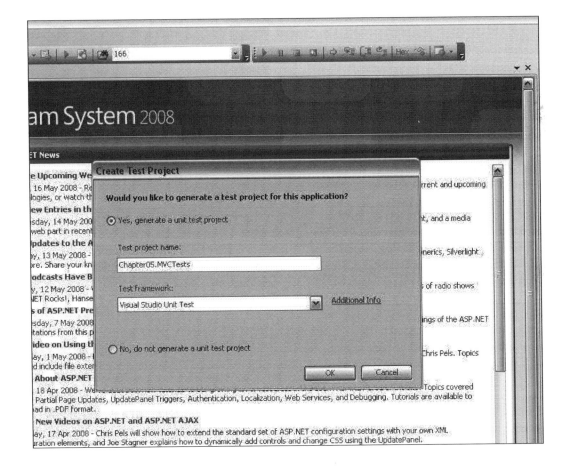

Select the default option and click **OK**. You will notice that two projects have been added to the solution that VS has created. The first project is a web project where you'll implement your application. The second is a testing project that you can use to write unit tests against.

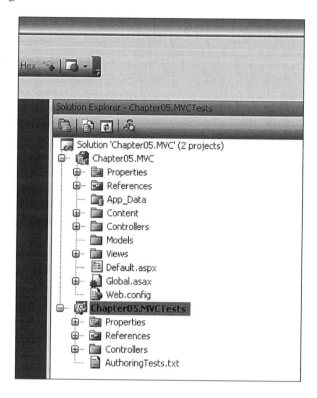

In our custom MVC code project, we had different projects (class libraries) for the model, the view, and the controllers.

The default directory structure of an ASP.NET MVC Application has three top-level directories:

- /Controllers
- /Models
- /Views

When the project becomes large, it is recommended that the Model, Views and Controllers are put in separate class library projects of their own so that it's easy to maintain them. But for the purpose of illustrating the ASP.NET MVC framework, this default structure is fine for us.

We will create a simple customer management application. For this, we first create some ASPX pages in the `Views` folder. Note that VS has already created these subfolders for us, under `Views`:

- **Home:** Contains the and Index views
- **Shared:** Contains shared views such as master pages

Before we go on to adding custom code in this project, let us understand what VS has done for us while creating this MVC project.

URL Routing Engine

In the standard ASP.NET model (or Postback model), the URLs map directly to the physical files:

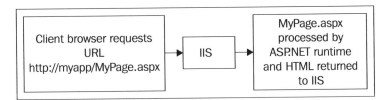

So when we make a request to a page, say `MyPage.aspx`, the runtime compiles that page and returns the generated HTML back to IIS to be displayed by the client browser. So we have a one-to-one relationship between the application URLs and the page.

But in the MVC framework, the URLs map to the controller classes.

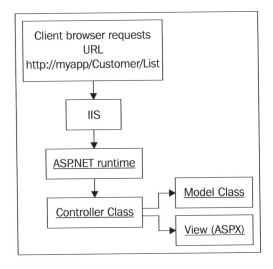

Therefore, the URL is sent to IIS and then to ASP.NET runtime, where it initiates a controller class based on the URL, using the URL routes, and the controller class then loads the data from the model, with this data finally being rendered in the view.

The controller classes uses URL routing to map the URLs, which in simpler terms means rewriting URL. We can set up the rules for which URL is to be routed to which controller class. The routing will pick up the appropriate controller and pass in the query string variables as necessary.

Open the `global.asax.cs` file and examine the following code:

```
public class GlobalApplication : System.Web.HttpApplication
    {
        public static void RegisterRoutes(RouteCollection routes)
        {
            routes.IgnoreRoute("{resource}.axd/{*pathInfo}");
            routes.MapRoute(
                "Default",
// Route name
                "{controller}/{action}/{id}",
// URL with parameters
                new { controller = "Home", action = "Index", id = "" }
}// Parameter defaults
            );
        }
        protected void Application_Start()
        {
            RegisterRoutes(RouteTable.Routes);
        }
```

The `RegisterRoutes()` method contains the URL mapping routes. Initially we have only the default rule set:

```
            routes.MapRoute(
                "Default",
// Route name
                "{controller}/{action}/{id}",
// URL with parameters
                new { controller = "Home", action = "Index", id = "" }
// Parameter defaults
            );
```

This URL mapping engine comes from `System.Web.Routing.dll`, which can be used independently, without the ASP.NET MVC framework, to rewrite URLs in your standard ASP.NET web applications.

The `MapRoute()` method, which handles URL routing and mapping, takes three arguments:

- Name of the route (string)
- URL format (string)
- Default settings (object type)

In our case, we named the first route "Default" (which is the route name) and then set the URL as:

```
Controller/action/id
```

The `Controller` here is the name of the controller class. `action` will be the method that needs to be invoked inside that controller class. `id` would be the parameters that need to be passed, if any.

In the default arguments, we create a new object and call it "Home", set the action to Index, and do not pass parameters to it. Note the new anonymous type syntax used to create parameter defaults:

```
new { controller = "Home", action = "Index", id = "" }
```

The var keyword and anonymous types: We normally use classes to wrap behavior and properties, but in C# 3.0, we can create the types anonymously without needing to create classes for them. This can be useful when we need to create light weight classes that have only read-only properties. We can use the anonymous syntax to create those types without the need to create a class for them. We can use the new "var" keyword to hold such anonymous types, for example:

```
var ch = new { readOnlyProperty1 = value1,
readOnlyProperty2 = value2 };
```

It is important that we name and assign a value to each of the properties that we are creating. What will be the type of the properties? They will automatically be cast to the data types of the values of the properties specified. The anonymous types will always be derived from the base object class directly. They can only be used within class members and cannot be passed as method arguments (unless they are boxed), return values, or be specified as class-level variables. Once the type is created, it cannot be changed into another type.

So we create a new anonymous type as the last argument of the `MapRoute()` method, passing in variable defaults with three properties, namely controller, action, and parameter.

Now have the `Default.aspx` page under the root directory, which acts as a redirecting page to the main home page of the site (which is `/View/Home/Index.aspx`).

We cannot directly set that as the "default" page since we are using URL routes to process pages instead of using physical files in the URLs.

So in the code-behind of our `Default.aspx` page, we have a simple redirect:

```
public void Page_Load(object sender, System.EventArgs e)
    {
          Response.Redirect("~/Home");
    }
```

So the runtime will first set up routes in the `global.asax` page, then it will process the `Default.aspx` page. Here it faces a redirect to this URL: `/Home`.

The Controller

The MVC framework maps this URL to the route set in the global route table, which currently has only the default one, in this format:

`Controller/action/id`

So `/Home` corresponds to a controller named Home, and because we have not specified any action or ID, it takes the default values we specified in the `RegisterRoutes()` method in the `globals.asax.cs`. So the default action was Index and the default parameter was an empty string. The runtime initializes the `HomeController.cs` class, and fires the Index action there:

```
public class HomeController : Controller
    {
          public ActionResult Index()
          {
              ViewData["Title"] = "Home Page";
              ViewData["Message"] = "Welcome to ASP.NET MVC!";
              return View();
          }}
```

In this `Index()` method, we set the data to be displayed in the View (aspx/ascx pages) by using a dictionary property of the base Controller class named `ViewData`. `ViewData`, as the name suggests, is used to set view-specific data in a dictionary object that can hold multiple name/value pairs. When we call the `View()` method, the `ViewData` is passed by the Controller to the View and rendered there.

The View

Let us now look at the View. How does the framework know which View or aspx page to call? Remember that we passed the value "Index" in the action parameter (in the default route in the `global.asax.cs` file), so the `Index.aspx` will get called. Here is the code-behind of `Index.apsx`:

```
public partial class Index : ViewPage
    {
    }
```

There is absolutely no code here, which is a very important characteristic of the MVC design. The GUI should have no logical or data fetching code. Note that the `Index` class is derived from the `ViewPage` class. Using this `ViewPage` class, we can access all of the items in the `ViewData` dictionary that were set in the controller's `Index()` method and passed on to the View. Here is how we are accessing the `ViewData` in HTML:

```
<asp:Content ID="indexContent" ContentPlaceHolderID="MainContent"
                runat="server">
    <h2><%= Html.Encode(ViewData["Message"]) %></h2>
    <p>
        To learn more about ASP.NET MVC visit <a href="http://asp.net/
mvc" title="ASP.NET MVC Website">http://asp.net/mvc</a>.
    </p>
</asp:Content>
```

We can directly access the `ViewData` dictionary in HTML. Now that we have seen how MVC works, we will create a new page to learn how to show data using a custom DAL and strongly typed objects, instead of the `ViewData` dictionary. Our example page will show a list of all the customers.

The Model

We will use the 5-Tier solution we created in the previous chapter and change the GUI layer to make it follow the MVC design using the ASP.NET MVC framework. Open the solution we created in the previous chapter and delete the ASP.NET web project from it. The solution will then only contain `5Tier.BL`, `5Tier.DAL` and `5Tier.Common` projects.

Right click the solution in VS, and select **Add New Project**, and then select **ASP.NET MVC Web Application** from the dialog box. Name this new web project as `Chapter05.MVC`. This web project will be the new MVC based UI tier of our OMS application in this chapter.

The `Customer.cs` and `CustomerCollection.cs` class files in the business tier (5Tier. Business class library) will be the Model in our MVC application. To show a list of customers, the `CustomerCollection` class simply calls the `FindCustomer()` method in `CustomerDAL.cs`. We have already seen these classes in action in the previous chapter. So we can use an n-tier architecture in an MVC application, hence this shows that MVC and n-tier are not mutually exclusive options while considering the application architecture of your web application. Both actually compliment each other.

We can also create a utility class named `CustomerViewData` to transfer the Model objects to the View. There are multiple ways to pass- in the Model to the View through the Controller, and creating `ViewData` classes is one of them. Here is the `CustomerViewData` class created in the `CustomerComtroller.cs` file in the `Chapter05.MVC` web project:

```
#region ViewData
        /// <summary>
        /// Class used for transferring data to the View
        /// </summary>
        public class CustomerViewData
        {
            public CustomerViewData() { }
            public CustomerViewData(Collection<Customer> customers)
            {
                this.customers = customers;
            }
            public Collection<Customer> customers;
            public Customer customer;
        }
        #endregion
```

Notice that this `ViewData` class is simply wrapping the business object inside it so that we can use this class in the UI layer instead of directly passing and manipulating domain objects.

Wiring Controller, Model, and View

We will now create routes in the `global.asax` file under the existing home page route as follows:

```
routes.MapRoute(
"Customer", "Customer/{action}/{id}", new {
 controller = "Customer", action = "Show", id="" } );
```

This new route will simply fire the Show action in the customer controller.

Now we create the controller class, `CustomerController`, as:

```
using NTier.BL;
using NTier.Common;
namespace Chapter05.MVC.Controllers
{
    public class CustomerController:Controller
    {
        #region ViewData
        /// <summary>
        /// Class used for transferring data to the View
        /// </summary>
        public class CustomerViewData
        {
            public CustomerViewData() { }
            public CustomerViewData(Collection<Customer> customers)
            {
                this.customers = customers;
            }
            public Collection<Customer> customers;
            public Customer customer;

        }
        #endregion
        public ActionResult Show()
        {
            CustomerViewData customerViewData = new CustomerViewData();
            CustomerCollection customers = new CustomerCollection();
            customerViewData.customers
            = customers.FindAll(LoadStatus.Loaded);
            return View("Show", customerViewData);
        }
    }//end class
}//end namespace
```

In this class, we first create a subclass called `CustomerViewData`, which is a wrapper to hold the `Customer` and `CustomerCollection` business objects. We will transfer this class object to the actual view through the controller as:

```
public ActionResult Show()
    {
        CustomerViewData customerViewData = new CustomerViewData();
        CustomerCollection customers = new CustomerCollection();
        customerViewData.customers
        = customers.FindAll(LoadStatus.Loaded);

        return View("Show", customerViewData);
    }
```

In this controller action, we simply get the list of customers from the database and pass it to the `Show.aspx` page using the `View()` method.

To create the `aspx` pages, we will create a folder named `Customers` under the `View`, and add an `aspx` file named `Show.aspx` that will display a list of all the customers.

```
<asp:Content ID="Content1" ContentPlaceHolderID="MainContent"
runat="server">
    <asp:Repeater ID="rptCustomer" runat="server">
        <ItemTemplate>
            <%# Eval("Name")%>
        </ItemTemplate>
    </asp:Repeater>
</asp:Content>
```

In the code-behind, we simply bind the data as:

```
using System.Web.Mvc;
namespace Chapter05.MVC.Views.Customer
    {
        public partial class Show :
         ViewPage <Controllers.CustomerController.CustomerViewData>
        {
            protected void Page_Load(object sender, EventArgs e)
            {
            rptCustomer.DataSource = ViewData.Model.customers;
            rptCustomer.DataBind();
            }
        }
    }
```

So the code-behind is kept very light and has no extra code besides data binding to the repeater. Note that usually in the standard postback model, we bind the data under the `if(!IsPostBack)` condition so that data binding happens only once, on the page load, and not on the postback.

Here we cannot follow the same pattern as there is no concept of a postback in MVC. Each request will be as unique as the RESTful URL.

If we want, we can also bind the data in the ASPX using inline code without using code-behind, as shown here:

```
<h2>Customer list</h2>
    <%foreach (var c in ViewData.Model.customers) { %>
        <div>
        <%=c.Name %>
        <br />
        </div>
    <%} %>
```

Note the use of the "var" type to get the `CustomerData` object. This helps us in avoiding explicit casting to get the `Customer` object.

In the same way, we can edit and add objects. An important point to note is that we don't need to use the standard ASP.NET button controls any more, because we don't want the page to postback to itself. Instead, when we add a customer, we can use something like this:

```
<form method="post" action="Customer/Add">
    <input type="text" name="customerName" value="" />
    <input type="submit" name="Add" value="Add" />
</form>
```

Notice that there is no `runat="server"` tag here in these controls as they are not server controls but simple HTML controls. On clicking the **Add** button, the page will post with the action `Customer/Add`. This means that, in the `CustomerController`, it will fire the `Add` method as shown in the sample code (just for demonstration purposes):

```
public class CustomerController : Controller
    {
    public ActionResult Add(string customerName)
        {
        //create a business object and fire the add method
        Customer customer = new Customer();
        customer.Name = customerName;
        CustomerCollection customers = new CustomerCollection();
        customers.Add(customer);
        return View("Home");
        }
    }
```

ASP.NET MVC will automatically set the parameter, `customerName`, with the value of the textbox from the form's post data, and will pass this value in the `Add` method of the controller. So we did not have to create the entire page object again, as the page did not postback to the same form. Hence, we avoided recreating the page class on every request or postback.

Because this chapter is more about understanding the MVC framework from the architecture's perspective, we will not go into the details of the edit and add actions; it is best to refer to the following post for these details:

```
http://weblogs.asp.net/scottgu/archive/2007/12/09/asp-net-mvc-
framework-part-4-handling-form-edit-and-post-scenarios.aspx
```

Unit Testing and ASP.NET MVC

Unit testing is the process where the developer himself tests the code that he has written. The word "unit" here refers to modules of code that he writes, such as methods, functions, and so on. The developer would test such "units" code to verify whether everything is working as expected. This will make sure that at least the individual methods of a class work without errors. Unit testing is different from the function or integration testing that a QA (quality assurance) person performs on a working model after the development phase is over. Unit testing is more closely related to the actual code testing and ensures that most of the bugs are taken care of before the project reaches the actual testing stage. Because unit testing checks the actual methods in the code, it can easily be automated by creating mock test cases in the code using one of the many available unit testing frameworks, such as NUnit and MBUnit.

Earlier in this chapter, we stressed the need for unit testing the GUI of our ASP.NET projects, and how difficult it is to do so under the standard page controller model. But now with ASP.NET MVC, we have "thin" code-behind classes, with almost little or no code. There are almost no Session and ViewState related issues, as all URLs are handled directly by the central controller. There are no button clicks, no code-behind event handlers, and so on. So it is easy to set up unit test cases for the controller classes because then it is the same as testing any normal C# class methods, such as the DAL, the BL, and so on.

Summary

ASP.NET MVC is a very good platform for creating unit-testable applications that are maintainable in the long run, as well as for achieving a clearer separation between the UI and the UI-handling logic. In the previous chapter, we learnt the n-tier architecture, but the GUI in such an architecture was still not easily testable as we had a lot of embedded UI code in code-behind classes that was dependent on ViewState and postbacks. But in MVC, the concept of ViewState and postback does not exist as each request is unique in and of itself. This also presents some technical challenges if you have a complex UI, such as a GridView with inline edit or update functionality with a lot of AJAX functionality, where MVC may not work as expected (though the upcoming ASP.NET MVC framework releases will offer more flexible solutions to handle such cases).

Also, server controls such as `DropDownList` may not work as expected in the ASP.NET MVC framework, since there would be no control-level events in the code-behind and the control won't be able to postback. The core principle of the ASP.NET MVC framework is that the URL should talk directly to the requested resource in the web application. This is also the core principle of REST. So if we are using control-level events such as the `selected_change()` method of a `DropDownlist` in code-behind to process some logic, we will be breaking this very REST/MVC principle. The reason is that during such an event, the form will postback without any change in the URL, hence the concept of REST will not hold true (remember that a resource on the web can be accessed by a unique RESTful URL). ASP.NET MVC also has an out-of-the-box powerful URL rewriting capability so that we can have SEO friendly URLs in our application.

This implies that the entire page lifecycle will have no value in the MVC framework. Using MVC means going back to using standard HTML controls instead of rich server controls (even though Microsoft is coming up with a separate set of MVC server controls which will help us in adopting MVC in our applications easily).

The ASP.NET MVC framework was still evolving during the time of writing of this book. There can be a lot of upcoming improvements in the framework in terms of added functionalities and utilities. These changes will cause the final ASP.NET MVC framework release to be somewhat different in terms of syntax shown in this chapter. But the core principle of MVC will remain the same and it will be quite easy to use the latest framework release once we understand the basic principles of the MVC design.

Using MVC in real world commercial applications needs more skill than using the standard ASP.NET postback model. But it gives us the unique benefit of unit testing the GUI layer along with the BL and the DAL, which really helps in Test Driven Development (TDD). So, the ASP.NET MVC framework is not a silver bullet, and you should carefully consider when and in which projects to use it. There will also be a learning curve associated with it for developers coming from a webforms background. It is not a replacement for webforms, but now developers have a choice of using either the MVC or the standard webforms page-centric postback model. ASP.NET MVC can easily be used with an n-tier architecture, as we saw in our code sample.

So ASP.NET MVC is a very good choice for creating a unit-testable and search engine friendly web application which makes our web UI much cleaner by having a clear separation between the UI and code logic.

6
Design Patterns

In the first chapter of this book, we learned that a design pattern is a re-usable solution that can be used in our projects so that time-tested programming techniques can be employed to solve similar kinds of problems. This chapter is devoted exclusively to design patterns and how we can use some of the famous design patterns in our ASP.NET web applications.

In the previous chapters we have already studied some design patterns such as:

- **Lazy Loading design pattern**: This is used to defer the loading of object properties until needed. This pattern helped us improve performance as data was only loaded when required.
- **Page controller design:** This is used to move the programming logic from markup to code-behind controller files for better code management.
- **Front controller design:** This is a centralized controller based approach to get rid of issues with page controller approach.
- **MVC design:** This is a powerful pattern used to separate the view from logic based on a front controller based design

In this chapter, we will focus on the following:

- Understanding different categories of design patterns
- Implementing the Singleton pattern
- Implementing the Factory pattern
- Understanding and implementing Dependency Injection
- Understanding the Command Design Pattern

Understanding Design Patterns

Design patterns not only help us to solve problems, but also gives us an assurance that the solutions will work and are stable, because these patterns have been tried and tested over the years by many other programmers. As we read earlier, design patterns are simple, and provide the best solutions to some of the common problems that developers face. Hence, they are more reliable than an ingenious solution to a problem that may have already been solved by others.

Any software problem can have many solutions, as depicted by the following diagram:

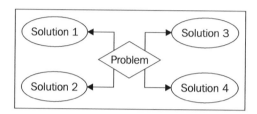

Some of these solutions might be innovatively new and use creative methods of finding an approach and a possible answer to a problem. Some solutions might be workable but not efficient. When it comes to deciding for the best approach for our current problem, we should first try to learn from the past, and understand how similar problems might have been solved by others. This is where **design patterns** come into picture.

History of Patterns

Much of the foundation of the design patterns was laid down by the "**Gang of Four**" (**GoF**)—Erich Gamma, Richard Helm, Ralph Johnson and John Vlissides, in their famous book "Design Patterns". The Gang of Four categorized design patterns into three groups:

- Creational
- Structural
- Behavioral

Creational patterns deal with different ways of creating an object to suit a particular scenario. One of the famous examples is the factory design pattern.

Structural patterns are related to the way in which a group of objects should be structured to achieve a goal, and how the relationships should be maintained between different objects. The Adapter pattern is a well known example of structural design pattern.

Behavioral patterns are related to how the objects co-ordinate and communicate with each other. The Command design pattern is a famous behavioral pattern.

An important point to note is that sometimes a design pattern may use some other design patterns to solve a particular problem. So a design pattern is not atomic in nature but may comprise of multiple patterns. Also, there is no strict rule when following a design pattern, which means you don't need to copy it word-for-word, or code-by-code. A design pattern is just an approach that has worked well in similar cases for other developers. Not all situations or programming problems are the same. Hence, if we are following a particular design pattern we might need to modify it to suit our custom needs, instead of blindly following it verbatim.

There are a lot of design patterns, and discussing all of them is beyond the scope of this book. So we will focus only on a few important, basic ones that every developer must be aware of when developing web applications in ASP.NET.

Singleton Pattern

Singleton is a creational design pattern that helps us restrict and control the number of objects instantiated for a particular class throughout the application life cycle. In this section, we will understand this design pattern by examining some example code. Singleton is one of the most widely used patterns in ASP.NET.

A common programming problem is to create a single instance of an object and make sure that there are no other instances except this single instance. Only this instance should serve all incoming requests and communicate with other objects. The Singleton pattern is a design pattern that can be used to implement such scenarios.

There may be numerous programming scenarios when we may need to restrict an object to a single instance. Some of them are:

- A single instance of a mail server might be required to process all incoming mail requests.
- The `Session` object in ASP.NET is implemented using singleton pattern. That is why each user will have only one session instance accessible at any point of time.
- The `Application` object in ASP.NET is also singleton based. There is only one instance of the `Application` object for an entire application.
- We may need a single instance of a logging utility to process all logging requests in our application.

The ASP.NET framework itself implements a singleton pattern. Besides, in the `Session` object, the singleton pattern can be seen in the way a framework handles the worker process. We have one and only one instance of the work process catering to all incoming HTTP requests.

Understanding Singleton with Code Example

Let's understand the Singleton pattern with the help of an example. In our OMS application, we have many orders coming in, and we want all customers to be notified whenever they place an order. For this, we have an `EmailManager` class. This class has the responsibility to send emails to all customers who have placed orders. Now, because ASP.NET is multi-threaded (it creates a new thread for each new client request), if we start creating a new instance of the `EmailManager` (as in `EmailManager em = new EmailManager()`) to process emails, we will have a lot of such instances, for multiple requests. In simple terms, if 50 customers placed their orders through the web site, we will have 50 instances of the `EmailManager` object. So let's assume that the requirement is to handle all emails in one instance and avoid having many instances as this might have a performance impact on server memory.

 Ideally, we should have a separate email application which would be handling all of these application-related emails. There can be different ways of handling emails in different applications. However, for the purpose of understanding design patterns, we will assume that we have to use Singleton to restrict the creation of `EmailManager` instances in our application.

So how can we make sure that there is one and only once instance of the `EmailManager` class throughout the life of our application? One approach is the use of **Static classes** in ASP.NET. Static classes are defined using the `static` keyword and the .NET compiler makes sure that there is no instance of a static class, and its methods can be called without creating any instance, as in:

```
public static EmailManager
{

    public static MyMethod()

    //other static methods

}
```

Now, the problem with this approach is that we cannot use static classes as method arguments and this might severely limit our scope. We may need to pass an instance of the EmailManager class to some other method, but with static classes we cannot do so.

Also, if we want to have different implementations of EmailManager created with different functionality, but with the same behavior (by using interfaces and then having different implementational classes), we will not be able to do that with static classes. Anyways, the singleton pattern is about ensuring that only a single "instance" of our class is always created, and to achieve this goal making our classes static is neither a good approach nor is it feasible in many cases. So let us look at a better approach.

The next strategy would be:

To use the singleton design pattern. The following code shows our class (this code is a stripped-down and simplified version; to have working code it is recommended that you follow the code provided in the code bundle):

```
public sealed class EmailManager
{
        private static EmailManager _manager;
    //Private constructor so that objects cannot be created
        private EmailManager()
        {
        }
        public static EmailManager GetInstance()
        {
          // Use 'Lazy initialization'
          if (_manager == null)
          {
            //ensure thread safety using locks
            lock(typeof(EmailManager)
            {
              _manager = new EmailManager();
            }
          }
        return _manager;
        }
}
```

Now let us understand the code step-by-step:

1. `public sealed class EmailManager`: We have used the `sealed` keyword to make our `EmailManager` class uninheritable. This is not necessary, but there is no use having derived classes as there can be only one instance of this class in memory. Having derived class objects will let us create two or more instances which will be against the singleton's design objective.

2. `private static EmailManager _manager`: Next, we create a variable named `_manager`, which holds a reference to the single instance of our `EmailManager` class. We have used a static modifier because we will be accessing this variable from a static method—`GetEmailManager()`, and static methods can use only static variables.

   ```
   private EmailManager()
         {

         }
   ```

   We need to create a private constructor to make sure that we don't accidentally initialize an object of the `GetEmailManager` class. By only initializing via the static `GetInstance()` method, we should get a single instance of this class.

3. ```
   public static EmailManager GetInstance()
   {
               // Use 'Lazy initialization'
         if (_manager == null)
               {
         //ensure thread safety using locks
         lock(typeof(EmailManager)
               {
                                 _manager = new EmailManager();
                     }
         }
               return _manager;
   }
   ```

   `GetInstance()` is the static method that we will use from outside this code to get the current reference of the `EmailManager` class. In this method, we are using the lazy loading technique (discussed in Chapter 4) to load the instance on demand. We first check if the current instance is null or not. If it is null, then we create a new one; otherwise we return the existing static instance.

   ```
   lock(typeof(EmailManager)
   ```
   ```

4. The `private _manager` object, marked `static`, is used inside a critical section (using `lock`) to make sure it is thread safe. Thread safety is very important here. Otherwise, two threads might simultaneously call `GetInstance()` and, on finding the `EmailManager` instance (`_manager`) null, will both try to create an instance, thereby creating two instances of the class. The `lock` keyword helps us make sure that once a thread enters the region, no other thread can do so until the first thread exits, making our code thread safe. We pass the `EmailManager`'s type in order to lock the statement using the `typeof` operator to define the scope of the lock statement.

An important point to note is that in the above code we have to make sure that the type used in the `typeof()` command is not publicly accessible, otherwise the scope would be affected. It is better to create a `private` object within our class to use as a reference object in the `lock` statement, as in:

```
private static object forLock = new object();
public static EmailManager GetInstance()
        {
                // Use 'Lazy initialization'
                if (_manager == null)
                {
        //ensure thread safety using locks
        lock(typeof(forLock)
            {
                                _manager = new EmailManager();
                    }
        }
            return _manager;
        }
```

So the above code can be used for implementing a Singleton design pattern in ASP.NET effectively and safely. Now we will move to another famous design pattern—the Factory method.

Factory Method

The Factory design pattern is another heavily-used pattern in ASP.NET applications to help introduce loose coupling and remove dependencies in the code. The Factory method is a creational design pattern that is used to create objects without any prior knowledge of the type of the object. We delegate the responsibilities of creating the actual objects to subclasses or separate factory classes. This can be accomplished by using interfaces or abstract classes.

Why do we need this design pattern? Change is one thing that we cannot avoid in software development. No matter how strictly we jot down specifications of the software we are making, there will always be some changes in the future. And each such change might affect the application code base. So there is no way of avoiding changes, and unless our applications are designed to adapt to these changes, we will be spending more time and money on changing the application code each time a change is requested. The factory design helps us make our applications "change-friendly".

Here is a representative class diagram showing how a Factory pattern might be used in an object model:

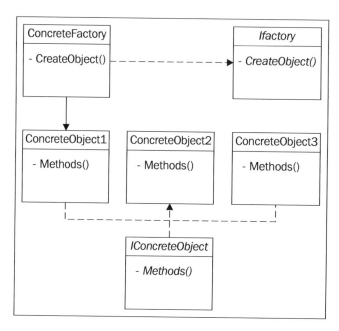

We have `IConcreteObject`, an interface to be implemented by all of the `ConcreteObject` classes. We use this interface to abstract all methods.

We have three concrete object classes implementing the `IConcreteObject`, `ConcreteObject1`, `ConcreteObject2`, and `ConcreteObject3` interfaces.

Now, we have an interface named `Ifactory` and the `ConcreteFactory` class is implementing that interface and is responsible for creating the concrete objects (`ConcreteObject1`, `ConcreteObject2`, or `ConcreteObject3`). It is up to the concrete factory as to which class is to be instantiated.

So the responsibility for creating the object is delegated to the `ConcreteFactory` class. Let us first understand the basic Factory design , through the use of a simple practical example.

Core Principle: Programming to an Interface instead of an Implementation

One of the core principles of object-oriented programming is to always program to an interface instead of a concrete object. Let us understand this in detail. Assume that we have multiple kinds of products in our OMS (Order Management System) such as foods, electronics and beauty products. To encapsulate these different products, we create different classes, such as FoodProducts, ElectronicProducts, BeautyProducts, and so on.

Because each product will have common properties and methods shared by all kinds of products, for example Unit Cost, Size, Weight, and so on, we create an interface called IProducts to list the basic behavior of a product.

```
public interface IProduct
{
        float UnitCost { get; set;}
        float Weight    {get; set;}

        bool Update();
}
```

In this interface-IProduct- we have defined two basic fields with both getter and setter properties, along with a method. (There can be more, but for the purpose of our understanding, we will work with only these two properties and one method.)

Next, we create individual concrete product classes (one for each different product). Here is one such class, BeautyProduct:

```
public class BeautyProduct:IProduct
{
   private float _unitCost;
   private float _weight;
   private int _forGender;
   public float UnitCost
   {
     get { return _unitCost; }
     set { _unitcost = value; }
   }

   public float Weight
   {
     get { return _ weight; }
     set { _ weight = value; }
   }
```

```
public int ForGender
  {
    get { return _ forGender; }
    set { _ forGender = value; }
  }


public bool Update()
{
 try
   {
     //code to update the product calling DAL method
     return ProductDAL.Update(this);
   }
  catch(Exception ex)
  {
      //log and rethrow...
  }
}
```

In the above concrete class, we have implemented the IProduct interface with concrete methods and properties. Note that we have added a property called ForGender, which tells us the gender group to which this beauty product belongs. This can be male, female or unisex, with each value being represented by an integer, as in 1, 2, or 3.

Because this is a beauty product specific property, it is not present in the interface, IProduct.

Now if we want to use BeautyProduct objects in our code, the first and simple approach would be:

```
BeautyProduct bp = new BeautyProduct();
```

Let us understand this line in more detail. The new keyword is used to create a new instance of a class. When using the new keyword, there are two important points to consider — the "type" of the object on the left-side and the right-side of the new keyword. In the above case, we are programming to a concrete implementation, that is, BeautyProduct, so the type of the object bp is BeautyProduct, and the implementation type is also BeautyProduct (as we have used in this syntax, new BeautyProduct()).

The problem with this method of using an object is that there is no flexibility, and the objects are tightly coupled with their class types. For example, we might need to use the Product object in different cases, as we might have a ProductManager class that will create and return a product to be added in an OrderLineItem object (this class will return an appropriate product object based on the type of product a customer has ordered). The following is a sample code of such a ProductManager class that returns a BeautyProduct object:

```
public class ProductManager
{
  //misc. methods to handle products
  //
  public BeautyProduct OrderProduct()
    {
BeautyProduct bp = new BeautyProduct();
//set bp properties
bp.OrderDate = Datetime.Now;
//reset the product count in the inventory as this product has been
//ordered
bp.ResetInventory();
return bp;
    }
}
```

In the above code sample, we have the OrderProduct() method that creates a new instance of BeautyProduct, and returns it to the consuming class (which might use this object to perform operations on it, as in an Order class).

> We will not be focusing on other methods in the Product/ ProductManager class that are related to handling and applying business logic related methods and properties, as our main focus is to understand the approach to solve problems in a better way by using design patterns!

The problem with this way of programming is that it makes our application too rigid, because to create another type of product object, say ElectronicProduct, we need to write another OrderProduct method in the ProductManager class. The ProductManager class returns an object of type, ElectronicProduct, which looks something like this:

```
public ElectronicProduct OrderEletronicProduct()
    {
ElectronicProduct ep = new ElectronicProduct ();
//set ep properties
ep.OrderDate = Datetime.Now;
```

```
//reset the product count in the inventory as this product has been
//ordered
ep.ResetInventory();
return ep;
}
```

So for each type of product, we need to add multiple order methods with different return signatures, which is quite messy. Also, in future, if we add a new type of product, we need to open our `ProductManager` class and modify it to make sure it can create and return the new product type. So this approach makes our code very rigid, inflexible and open to modifications each time there is a change. To avoid this, we can use **Polymorphism** and **program to interfaces** instead of using the concrete classes.

So what does 'programming to interfaces' mean? We create an object using the interface/super class as the type instead of the concrete classes. This means:

```
BeautyProduct bp = new BeautyProduct();
```

becomes

```
IProduct bp = new BeautyProduct();
```

Note that the type of the bp object is now the interface, making it possible for us to switch to different concrete types during code execution. This is known as **Runtime polymorphism**. Let us see how we can use this approach to make our `ProductManager` class better:

```
public class ProductManager
{

public IProduct OrderProduct()
  {

//misc. methods
IProduct bp = new BeautyProduct();
//set bp properties
bp.OrderDate = Datetime.Now;
//reset the product count in the inventory as this product has been
//ordered
bp.ResetInventory();
      return bp;
   }
}
```

Now, because we have used IProduct in the method signature, we can pass in all current and future concrete implementation classes in this method as long as they implement the IProduct interface:

```
IProduct  p = new EletronicProduct();
return p;
```

Also, programming to interfaces gives us the flexibility of **Dynamic polymorphism**. We don't have to worry about the type of concrete implementations, as they are all deriving from a common abstract class or implementing a common interface. There is something we avoid—writing multiple Create methods for different product types.

The Need for Factory Design

So far so good. But we still need to make sure that our OrderProduct method can return multiple product types. How does the code in OrderProduct() method know which concrete type to return? One option is that we modify the code so that it can include the type of the product passed as a second parameter. Then, by using a switch case or if else statements, we can have different creational logic implemented for each concrete type, as follows:

```
public IProduct OrderProduct(string productType)
  {
     IProduct product;
     switch(productType)
   {
   case "BeautyProduct": product = new BeautyProduct();
                         break;
   case "ElectronicProduct": product = new ElectronicProduct ();
                         break;
   case "FoodProduct": product = new FoodProduct ();
                         break;
   default: break;
     }
//set product properties
product.OrderDate = Datetime.Now;
//reset the product count in the inventory as this product has been
//ordered
product.ResetInventory();

  return product;
  }
```

As you can see, we now face another issue. If we add a new product in future, we will still need to modify our OrderProduct method to add another switch case statement for the newly-added product, so that OrderProduct can return it.

To fix this issue, and to make our code more elegant and flexible, we need to abstract the product creation logic to some other class. This is where the factory design can help us.

We take the product creation code out of the ProductManager class and create a new class to handle and return the correct type of product object. So the only role of this new class would be to create and return product objects based on the object type passed to it. This will make our ProductManager class independent of handling the correct product type and allow it to focus on other important business rules that may need to be applied for managing products.

We will call this class ProductFactory. Here is the code for that class:

```
public class ProductFactory
{
  public IProduct CreateProduct(string productType)
  {
    IProduct product = null;
    switch(productType)
  {
  case "BeautyProduct": product = new BeautyProduct();
                      break;
  case "ElectronicProduct": product = new ElectronicProduct ();
                      break;
  case "FoodProduct": product = new FoodProduct ();
                      break;
  default: break;
    }
  return product;
  }
}
```

This factory class takes the product type as a string parameter and simply returns the appropriate concrete product object based on this parameter. Here is how our ProductManager will use this factory class:

```
public class ProductManager
{
ProductFactory factory= new ProductFactory();
IProduct product;
 //misc. methods to handle products
public IProduct OrderProduct(string productType)
```

```
    {
product   = factory.CreateProduct(productType);
//set product properties
product.OrderDate = Datetime.Now;
//reset the product count in the inventory as this product has been
//ordered
product.ResetInventory();
return product;
    }
}
```

In the above code, the `ProductFactory` class has abstracted the product creation logic. So if there are new products to be added in future, we don't need to change the code in the `ProductManager` class; only the `factory` class needs to be changed. We have de-coupled the `ProductManager` class and made it more flexible by adding another level of indirection in terms of a `factory` class.

Another example where you will find factory design useful is when you want your application to be able to talk to different database types. You may not know which database each of your clients (to whom you sold your application) has. It could be MS SQL Server, Oracle, FireBird, PostGres, or MySql.

You have developed the data access layer classes for each of these databases in your application code. Now you want your application to be able to instantiate any of the DAL classes based on the actual customer database. Our application does not know beforehand which database will be used. For such cases, and similar scenarios, the factory design pattern can help.

We will see another slightly different, real world, practical example of a Factory design in the next design pattern, **Dependency Injection (DI)**.

Dependency Injection

The Dependency Injection and factory design patterns are very common, and provide great flexibility in software development. Although most programmers have come across these patterns, they may not grasp the concepts completely until they see these patterns in action in real projects.

In this section, we will learn how to achieve loose coupling and "plug-and-play" architecture using these patterns, with the help of a sample project—a flexible encryption program. We will be focusing on the code from the viewpoint of understanding the Dependency Injection design pattern. Therefore, the detailed syntax and complete code will not be listed here. A complete working code for this example is provided in the code bundle.

The Dependency Injection (DI) design pattern is "a form of" the **Inversion of Control (IoC)** design which is applied in many frameworks. DI gives the flexibility of attaching a custom implementation such as a "plugin", without modifying existing software. Dependency Injection can be achieved using Constructor, Setter, or Interface Injection. In this chapter, we will learn and understand Interface Injection, which is quite common and more flexible than the other two approaches.

Basic Approach

We will follow a set of steps to achieve Dependency Injection in our working sample, as described below.

Step 1: Create an Interface

Let us start with our encryption program by authoring an interface so that others can implement their own algorithmic implementations by defining these methods in their own custom way:

```
public interface IEncryptionAlgorithm
{
    string Password
    {
        get;
        set;
    }
    byte[] RawInput
    {
        get;
        set;
    }

    byte[] Salt
    {
        set;
    }

    int KeySize
    {
        set;
    }
    byte[] Encrypt();
    byte[] Decrypt();
    bool CheckPassword();
}
```

In the above code, we have created an interface named IEncryptionAlgorithm, which will abstract the basic properties that every concrete algorithm needs to implement. This interface is a kind of a contract which the implementation classes need to follow for writing custom encryption methods. We have:

- Password: the password/key for each encryption algorithm
- RawInput: a byte array which will hold the data that needs to be encrypted
- Salt: salt is needed to make sure that our encryption code is harder to crack
- Keysize: the bigger the key size, the tougher it is to break the encryption
- Encrypt() method: returns the data as a byte array after encrypting it
- Decrypt() method: decrypts already-encrypted data back to the original data
- CheckPassword(): for demonstration purposes, we will be storing the password inside the encrypted data instead of some external location. So this method will be used before the actual decryption to check if the password entered by the user is correct or not.

Step 2: Create an Implementation

We first created an XOR based XOREncryption class, which implemented this interface:

```
public class XOREncryption : IEncryptionAlgorithm
```

We will implement the encryption and decryption methods along with the properties; for detailed code refer the code bundle. Here is the trimmed -0 down version:

```
public byte[] Encrypt()
{
    byte[] encryptedBytes = new byte[_rawInput.Length];
    byte[] keyBytes = ASCIIEncoding.ASCII.GetBytes(_key);
    //hard coded salt value
    _salt = new byte[] {0x11, 0x78, 0x22, 0xFF, 0xAC, 0x5C,
                        0x78, 0x4E, 0x7D, 0x45, 0xEF, 0xF1};
        //rest of the code goes here
}
```

We need to complete this class with other methods and properties defined by the interface (see the source code provided in the code bundle).

Step 3: Create another Implementation

Because we want to switch between multiple algorithmic implementations at runtime, we will create one more encryption algorithm implementation so that we can see the plug-n-play design in action:

```
public class RijndaelEncryption : IEncryptionAlgorithm
{
        //implement IEncryptionAlgorithm properties and methods
}
```

Now we have two implementations ready, and the question becomes how we dynamically instantiate one of these in the GUI.

Step 4: Create a Factory Class

For that, we need to use the Factory design pattern and create a Factory class as follows:

```
public sealed class AlgorithmFactory
{
    private AlgorithmFactory()
    { }

    public static IEncryptionAlgorithm GetSpecifiedAlgorithm()
    {
        string algoType = System.Configuration.
                    ConfigurationSettings.AppSettings["algo"];
        IEncryptionAlgorithm algoInstance;
        if (string.IsNullOrEmpty(algoType))
        {
            goInstance = Activator.CreateInstance(Type.
                GetType("NeekProtect.XOREncryption,NeekProtect"))
                as IEncryptionAlgorithm;
        }
        else
        {
            algoInstance = Activator.CreateInstance(Type.
                    GetType(algoType)) as IEncryptionAlgorithm;
        }
         return algoInstance;
    }
}
```

This Factory class is responsible for creating and returning concrete implementations based on the algorithm of our choice (specified in the web. config file). This class is sealed, because it doesn't make sense to inherit it. Also, the constructor is private, so its instance cannot be created at all, and all methods are made static. Why static? Because AlgorithmFactory is behaving like a Helper class, helping the clients to get an instance of the appropriate Algorithm implementation class. See the static GetSpecifiedAlgorithm() method; it returns an instance of IEncryptionAlgorithm. This is where we see the important design principle—"Always program to interfaces". Because each encryption algorithm class implements IEncryptionAlgorithm, the supertype of each implementation is the same—IEncryptionAlgorithm. Hence, we don't need to worry about the actual implementation class as long as the class implements the same interface.

Step 5: Implement the Configuration Settings

Here is how we get the type specified in the application config file:

```
string algoType =
        System.Configuration.ConfigurationSettings.AppSettings["algo"];
```

In the config file, the following entry is made (under appSettings):

```
<add key="algo" value="NeekProtect.XOREncryption,NeekProtect"/>
```

In the value, we specify the fully qualified class name and the assembly name in which the class is present, separated by a comma. We need this entry as we will dynamically load the assembly using Activator.CreateInstance, as:

```
IEncryptionAlgorithm algoInstance;
algoInstance = Activator.CreateInstance(Type.GetType(algoTyp)) as
                IEncryptionAlgorithm;
```

 If no entry is specified in the config file, then the XOR Encryption class is used as the default (see the code for AlgorithmFactory). algoInstance is then returned to the client caller.

Let us now see the client, and how it uses this instance. The class EncryptionEngine is our client here:

```
/// <summary>
/// This class prepares the byte array and sets files and directories
/// to be encrypted and calls the relevant encryption/decryption
/// algorithm
/// </summary>
    public class EncryptionEngine
{ .... }
```

This class has a method `EncryptFile`, as follows:

```
private void EncryptFile(string fullPath, string password)
{
            IEncryptionAlgorithm x =
                        AlgorithmFactory.GetSpecifiedAlgorithm();
            x.Password = password;
            x.KeySize = 128;
            string ext = Path.GetExtension(fullPath);
            byte[] extByte = Encoding.ASCII.GetBytes(ext);
            byte[] inputByte = File.ReadAllBytes(fullPath);
            MemoryStream m = new MemoryStream();
            m.Write(inputByte, 0, inputByte.Length);
            m.Write(extByte, 0, extByte.Length);
            x.RawInput = m.ToArray();
            byte[] o = x.Encrypt();
            …..//other stuff
}
```

We call the `AlgorithmFactory`'s static method `GetSpecifiedAlgorithm()`, which returns an instance of the class specified in the `config` file. Here, we don't care how the instance is returned; we just need an instance of `IEncryptionAlgorithm` so that we can encrypt the input file. This is another example of programming to interfaces.

Step 6: Implement another Custom Algorithm

In the above code, there is no mention of the two encryption classes we have coded earlier: `XOREncryption` and `RijndaelEncryption`. We only use `IEncryptionAlgorithm` in this code, and this gives us the flexibility to use any custom algorithm as long as it implements `IEncryptionAlgorithm`.

Let's suppose a user installs our encryption program, and is not satisfied by the two default algorithms provided. Now he or she wishes to use the 3DES algorithm with the program. How can he or she do that?

The user will need to create their own `3DESEncryption` class and implement all of the methods and properties specified in the `IEncryptionAlgorithm` interface, as follows:

```
public class 3DESEncryption: IEncryptionAlgorithm
{
        //implement IEncryptionAlgorithm properties and methods
}
```

Now the user has to compile it and place the resultant assembly in the folder where our program is installed, which is probably something like this: `C:\Program Files\ PP\Encryption Program`.

In the same folder, the user has to open and edit the XML `configuration` file (usually this file is named as `App.GUI.exe.config`) and create/overwrite the value of the key `algo` as:

```
<add key="algo" value="MyCustomAlgo.3DESEncryption, MyCustomAlgo "/>
```

(For the sake of illustration, we have assumed the namespace to be `MyCustomAlgo`).

Now the Factory class will return this instance to be used in our encryption program. So we see how the "plugin" type functionality can be achieved by using the Dependency Injection, and users can build their own custom implementations and plug them into our program.

Command Design Pattern

The Command design pattern is used to decouple the calling object and the object that is being called, so that the calling object does not know how its request will be executed by the called object. Let us understand this with the help of an example.

Usually, in association or aggregation relationships, the object holding a reference to another object will communicate with this object by invoking a method on it. For example, in our OMS web application, the `AddEditCustomer.aspx.cs` page object has a reference to the `Customer` object (an association, as the `Customer` object is used locally). The page object loads a particular `Customer` object by calling a method on it, for example:

```
Customer customer = new Customer();
customer.Load(customerID);
```

So the page object is interacting with the customer object by issuing a command to it (`Load()`, in our case). This is how objects usually interact and communicate with each other — by invoking commands.

Decoupling the GUI completely from the BL

Now let's take another scenario. In Chapter 4, we saw how we can use a 5-tier configuration and introduce loose coupling into our projects. In the sample OMS code, we saw that the GUI and the BL were loosely coupled, but the GUI was dependent on the BL in the sense that we had a reference to the BL in our GUI code (using statements referring to the BL Tier). What if we want the BL and the GUI to be completely independent of each other, where there is not even a one way reference between the GUI and the BL. This means that the GUI will not call business layer objects directly, as it doesn't know anything about them. One way to make this happen is to add another level of indirection by adding another tier. We can call it the Service Layer. The GUI can refer to and call this new Service layer method, which sits in between the GUI and the Business Layer and handles the abstraction. Here, the GUI talks to the Service Layer, and the Service Layer in turn interacts with the Business Layer.

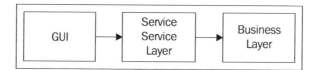

This decoupling will make our application more flexible as the GUI has no reference to the BL tier, and it does not need to know how the business logic will be handled. We can have multiple GUIs for the same business logic, and multiple business logic implementations for the same GUI. This complete independence makes software development much more flexible and robust, but also increases complexity.

In this scenario, assume that we are creating a GUI form to add a new customer. In the Add buttons click event handler, we cannot simply create a new Customer object because the GUI has no reference of the Customer class in the Business Layer. Additionally, it does not know which object would be there, and what methods that object would support. In such circumstances, we use the Command design pattern to abstract the invocation of the commands to associated objects.

Creating the Command Interface

In this design pattern, we create a Command object, which will encapsulate the actual command. Then the GUI will invoke this command object, which will issue the actual command. So a GUI object may be referred to as an "invoker" here, and the service layer would be the "receiver". First, we define an interface ICommand, and every concrete command implementation will implement this interface. This command infrastructure will help us decouple the GUI and the BL.

The ICommand interface will have only one method, Execute(), as follows:

```
public interface ICommand
    {
        CommandResult Execute(CommandArg cmdArg);
    }
```

Creating the Value Objects

Now we will create the different Command classes, which will implement this interface and actually be responsible for executing commands. Each command might need some arguments, and might return results as well. Because we will not be using custom objects here, we need to create generic wrappers to hold the arguments and the results. We will use the CommandArg class to hold the arguments, and the CommandResults class to hold the results.

Here is the code for the CommandArg class:

```
[Serializable]
public class CommandArg
    {
        private NameValueCollection _paramCollection=
                                        new NameValueCollection();

        public NameValueCollection ParamCollection
        {
          get
          {
            return _paramCollection;
          }
          set
          {
            _paramCollection=value;
          }
        }
    }
```

In this CommandArg class, we have a NameValueCollection (ParamCollection), which will wrap all of the command parameters (coming from the GUI) and their names, so that we can use them in the Service Interface layer.

Next, we will look at the CommandResults class, which will wrap the results after the command is executed, and then these results can be used by the UI layer.

```
[Serializable]
public class CommandResult
    {
        private object _scalarResult;
        private string _errorMessage="";

        public string ErrorMessage
        {
          get
```

```
        {
            return _errorMessage;
        }
        set
        {
            _errorMessage=value;
        }
    }
    public object ScalarResult
    {
        get
        {
            return _scalarResult;
        }
        set
        {
            _scalarResult=value;
        }
    }
}
```

This `CommandResult` class defines two properties:

- `ErrorMessage`: to wrap any error while the command is executed by the lower layers. This error can then be displayed accordingly in the GUI.

- `ScalarResult`: this property will wrap the results of the command execution in an object and then send this object to the UI layer.

Both of these objects would be common to both the GUI and the Service Interface layers, which are used to pass data along these layers. We can also use Data Transfer Objects here.

Now, we will see what the actual `Command` class that executes a command looks like:

```
public class GetCustomerCmd : ICommand
{
    public CommandResult Execute(CommandArg cmdArg)
    {

        CommandResult cmdResult = CustomerServiceInterface.
                                            GetCustomers(cmdArg);

        return cmdResult;
    }
}
```

In the above `GetCustomerCmd` class, the `Execute` method calls the `Service interface` object (we will define this in the next section), which in turn handles the business logic calls and returns the result in the `Command Result` object. The service interface method will refer to the BL layer, and use the BL objects to return the results. Here is a sample implementation:

```
public class CustomerServiceInterface
    {
        public CommandResult GetCustomers (CommandArg cmdArg)
        {
            CommandResult cmdResult = new CommandResult();
            CustomerCollection customers = new CustomerCollection();
            cmdArg = customer.FindCustomers(cmdArg);
            return cmdResult;
        }
    }
```

The service method above uses the `CustomerCollection` class from the BL layer, and calls the `FindCustomer` method by passing in the arguments. The FindCustomer method returns a list of `Customer` records. This list is returned by wrapping it in the `CommandResult class` object.

Creating the Command Factory

How will our interface know which command to execute? For this, we take the help of the Factory design pattern, and create a `CommandFactory` class. This class takes `eventName` as an argument and, based on this string, it creates the appropriate command.

Now, we will see how the `CommandFactory` class is implemented:

```
public class CommandFactory
    {
        public static ICommand CreateCommand(string eventName)
        {
            switch(eventName)
            {
                #region Customer Related
                    case "GetCustomer":
                    return new GetcustomerCmd();
                //other cases
                ...
            }
        }
    }
```

Here, we are returning the actual command based on the string `EventName`. Based on this string parameter, the Factory class returns a concrete command object to the caller. To make it more flexible, instead of using strings hard-coded in the code we can put them in an XML file, and load that file to create appropriate command objects.

Tying it all up with the GUI

In the `Addcustomer.aspx` GUI page code behind the file, we can simply use the following code to create a new customer:

```
ICommand command;
        // Call Create Command on CommandFactory passing EventName
        command = CommandFactory.CreateCommand("GetCustomer");
        CommandArg carg = new CommandArg();
        CommandResults results = null;
         carg.Add("customerID", "1");
        if (command !=null)
        {
           // Call Execute Method on Command Object.
           results  = command.Execute(cmdArg);
        }
    //bind results any data control or handle it
```

So we can clearly see that the GUI doesn't know anything about the Business Layer. All it does is create an instance of the command object by passing the required event name (`GetCustomer`) and then executing that command by passing arguments. The GUI doesn't need to know who handles the command and how the internal processing takes place. It just passes the required arguments on to the `Command` class, which then executes the command by talking to the business layer interface object.

This was just one example of how we can use the Command pattern to abstract the method invocation so that the caller does not need to worry about how the command will actually be executed. The example we studied is just one of the ways in which we can implement this pattern. However, each situation will need a different implementation, based on the actual needs although the basic principle would be same.

Summary

Design patterns not only save time and money, but also help you to build robust software, with the assurance that the solution has been tried and tested by many other developers over the years. In this chapter, we focused on a few of the common design patterns so that we can understand the principle behind them. There are many design patterns, and to know more about them, you can refer to any book dedicated to design patterns, for example *Design Patterns* by the Gang of Four.

No design pattern can be implemented as-is, because they are not bound by any implementation guidelines. They represent more of an *approach*, and often you will feel the need to modify and adapt a particular design pattern to fit your specific needs.

Using simple design patterns can help you to create flexible and robust software that is not only easy to maintain but also helps to reduce maintenance costs.

7
SOA and WCF

In the previous chapters, we covered a lot of interesting topics, such as:

- How layered and tiered architectures work
- How to implement an n-tier architecture in our web applications
- How to use the ASP.NET MVC framework to completely de-couple our UI from the code logic and make our GUI more unit-test friendly
- How to use design patterns to write better and more robust code

In this chapter, we will learn about another famous architecture, known as **Service Oriented Architecture (SOA)**. We will also see how we can implement SOA using the latest Microsoft programming framework for communication between inter-connected systems, known as **Windows Communication Foundation (WCF)**. This chapter is not intended to be a comprehensive overview of either SOA or WCF, but is intended to give developers a general idea of SOA-based architectures, and where WCF fits in to this.

This chapter covers the following topics:

- Understanding application size, scope and granularity
- What is SOA
- Why we need SOA
- SOA using Web Services
- What is Window Communication Foundation (WCF)
- How we can implement SOA using WCF

Understanding Application Size, Scope, and Granularity

Change is the only thing common to all software projects. No matter how perfect the architecture is, or how robust the code is, we cannot guarantee that the business needs will not change in the future. The core business logic may remain the same, but new "non-core" changes can arise, such as the introduction of new product items, modifications to data display routines, and so on. We cannot avoid change. A good architecture will adapt to change rather than fight it.

Requirement changes and modifications to the code, and their impact on the software application, depend on the actual scope and size of the application itself. So before we go ahead with examining how we can manage changes, we first need to understand how changes relate to the application's size and scope.

Small Applications Versus Big Applications

Web applications (or for that matter any kind of application that we may develop) can broadly be categorized as big or small.

If the application has limited scope in terms of size as well as complexity, then dealing with frequent changes in it, might be manageable. The developer working on such an application can quickly make changes and upload them—a process that will not take much time due to the limited scope and size of these web applications. Dealing with changes in a large application is altogether a different matter.

But how do we define or categorize applications as big or small? Here are some parameters that can help us define the scope of a web application. Applications can be categorized as "small", if they meet the following criteria:

- **Thin business rules:** The application's business logic is not complex, which means that the business layer is either too "thin" or non-existent (the web tier may talk directly with the data layer). For example, a simple website that has only a few tables in the database (possibly used for small forms such as "contact us" submissions), or a simple guestbook, or a simple time tracking application.

- **Limited inter-application communication:** The application does not need to talk with other external third-party applications in the same environment (say, within the same company, or within a network of computers, a LAN, and so on). An application can be labeled as "small", if it is not sharing and is not dependent upon other external applications. Examples of such a "small" application would be an e-card based website, or a small shopping cart in an e-commerce website.

- **Limited Future growth:** The Applications that don't need to grow with time, for example, a limited family album website, a small sports website, or an intra-company blog system.

- **Budget limitations:** Finally, one of the most important reasons for letting an application use a limited architecture and not increase its scope is money. A tiered scalable architecture is more complex, requires skilled programmers and takes more development time and hence more money. Often, project stakeholders (or clients) will not let an application use scalable architecture, as they want a quick turn-around time and less financial constraints. Hence, an application that might be categorized "big" according to the above criteria, would be limited in scope due to a limited budget.

Then there are big enterprise-level applications, which have wide scope across many verticals, and websites that may need to scale up in the future. Such big applications may depend on other third-party applications for updating, deleting or sharing data within the company. or even outside of it. In enterprise-level firms (big companies, such as those in the Fortune 1000), there are typically big software applications that collaborate with other applications, for example, accounting software may be integrated with **Enterprise Resource Planning** (**ERP**) software, or the Inventory system may be talking and sharing data with the financial software.

In such big systems, there can be a lot of inter-application communication, and because the number of users accessing these applications can grow with time, scalability, interoperability, and flexibility have to be built in. A small change in such applications can create a ripple effect and cause big changes in related systems.

So applications which are "small" in size and have a limited scope might get away with regular changes compared to large applications with complex business logic. Therefore, incorporating changes is quick and less costly. But in a large system, one change can break other applications that may be related to the system being changed. And the cost of making such changes is much more than in smaller systems, due to the complexity of the code base, and the possible impact on other applications within the same environment. Let us understand why the code base of such applications can get really complex making it difficult to incorporate future changes or modifications.

Tight and Fine-Grained Domain Model

Enterprise-level systems may have a very complex domain model, which contains lots of business classes and methods developed in an API-like fashion. In Chapter 4, we learnt that we could make our code base more flexible and adaptable to change by using an n-tier architecture with a proper domain model. But as our application grows in scope, this domain model itself might get very complex with deeply nested/related classes, thousands of methods and overloaded signatures, multiple parameters, and so on.

One way of measuring the complexity of an application is to understand the granularity of the application. Granularity defines the size of an application as well as the number of individual components in the system. For object-oriented software systems, we can use class methods as units of granularity. The more methods a class has, the more granular or fine-grained it is. Similarly, we can use the class itself as a measure of granularity. The more classes we have, the more fine-grained our system is. If it has less methods, then it is relatively coarse-grained (you can think of it in terms of currency; a $10 dollar note is coarse grained, and ten $1 notes are more fine-grained).

As we go along adding more functionality and classes to the system, the domain model may inflate to big proportions and become tightly intertwined, making it complex for use by external systems, and increasing the granularity of the system. Let us understand how.

Each class in such a business layer will have its own large set of methods with specific signatures, and in order to call these methods from outside the system (using an API), we need to provide all of the parameters in the method signature. For example, we can call a method to get a list of customers for a particular project, as in:

```
myAPIMethod.FindCustomers(int ProjectID, int pageNumber,
                          int pageLength, ref noOfPages);
```

Let's assume that the above code returns a paged list of all customers for a particular project ID, where `pageNumber` and `pageLength` denotes which page and how many records we want to return (as we want to show paged records). This method call is fine-grained because we are specifying each and every parameter to the business method call, which in turn passes these parameters to a data access layer (DAL) method and returns the results. We use the word "fine" here to denote the "exactness" of the method call, and if we leave out even one parameter, the method call will result in an error.

If we need to make changes in such fine-grained methods (for example, we might need to add a new parameter based on some new requirement), then all of our client programs that are using our API (also known as consumers of the API) will break down. These programs will need to change their code to pass in the modified method arguments so that our API works from within their code. This introduces tighter coupling between systems even in an n-tier architecture where the code might be used by other external programs.

To introduce loose coupling in such systems, we may sometimes use a coarse-grained model, which is described next.

Coarse-Grained Model

A coarse-grained model has fewer details , and in the context of an object-oriented system, coarse-grained means less classes and a limited number of methods, or methods with few parameters. For example, a coarse-grained version of the example class method discussed above, namely:

```
myAPIMethod.FindCustomers(int ProjectID, int pageNumber,
                          int pageLength, ref noOfPages);
```

will look like:

```
myAPIMethod.FindCustomers(int ProjectID);
```

As you can see, we removed the "fineness" of this method by removing the extra arguments, which were acting like "filters" on the data returned. So instead of getting only the specified number of paged results, we will get all the records of customers for a particular project ID. This means that the entire set is returned without any filter; hence it is a coarse-grained method when compared to the earlier method of passing paging-related parameters. We can make it even more coarse-grained by removing the project ID as the argument and returning all customers irrespective of the project to which they belong. The degree of coarseness or "fineness" depends on our actual project requirements.

So how is the granularity of the system related to flexibility and better change management? We will see this in the next section.

What is SOA?

SOA, or Service Oriented Architecture, is an architectural approach aimed at making it easy to introduce new features into an existing system, share data with other applications for easier integration, and bring a faster **Return On Investments (ROI)** to the business processes.

An important point to consider is that SOA does not formalize any approach or specific implementation technique. We can implement an SOA-based architecture using a number of different methods and approaches. SOA is an architectural guideline on how to achieve interoperability and cross-process integration in a scalable way. Most developers assume that SOA is equivalent to web services, but the fact is that web services are merely one of the convenient ways to implement an SOA-based architecture, due to the interoperability of XML across varied systems. But this does not imply that we cannot implement SOA without web services! If we don't have to communicate within a heterogeneous environment (having multiple platforms, software, and so on running across networks), then we can implement an SOA-like architecture using message-based systems and remoting. In a homogenous environment, web services may not be needed. But web services are the best options to use in an SOA because most enterprise systems that need to use SOA are operating in a heterogeneous environment.

A homogenous environment is the one where we have the same set of development platforms and operating system in all of the networked machines. For example, all machines within a company's internal LAN can have .NET runtime loaded with the Windows 2003 server. A heterogeneous environment is one where we have multiple Operating Systems running on different machines in the network. For example, we may have Windows on one, Linux on others, while some machines may have .NET runtime, and yet others may be hosting J2EE applications.

In this chapter, we will learn about SOA, and how it can help us achieve rapid application integration, code re-use, and automate business processes with the help of a practical example.

Why SOA?

We have been following OOAD, Object-Oriented Analysis and Design in the previous chapters, creating a domain model and using objects as the core framework for our applications. SOA does not make OOAD redundant; in fact, it complements it. OOAD is more of an implementation approach, whereas SOA is more of a high-level architectural approach.

In the previous chapters, we noticed that we used n-tier architecture to make our applications scalable, robust, and flexible. If n-tier architecture helps us build all of that, then why do we need SOA? The answer is: better change management!

As we saw earlier, we cannot avoid changes, and for large applications the domain model may become increasingly fine-grained and complex. Modifying such code to accommodate changes can become very complex, so the need was felt to have a solution that can help us take advantage of the domain model but manage changes in the long run without spending too much time and effort, and help keep our applications flexible and open for future modifications.

Service Orientation

Before understanding the term *service orientation*, let us consider a fictional scenario—Mr. Bhalla owns a small Marketing and Sales company with a few employees. Bhalla realized that his business and clients were growing quickly, and he was unable to handle all of the phone calls and paper work on his own. So he decided to hire an assistant who could do the basic office work, and handle paperwork and other office-related tasks for him. After some interviews he decided to select Ms. Akriti Katoch for the job. Mr. Bhalla was initially a bit skeptical as to whether Akriti could handle the work, so he decided to train her for some time. He told her that she simply needs to follow his instructions carefully. For example, to get a particular file, he would give her details of the file name, file color and the rack where it could be found. Similarly for each task set out to her, he would give her all of the details, so that she could work more efficiently.

For some time, everything went well. But after a while, Mr. Bhalla realized that giving Akriti all of the details was getting cumbersome. For example, if he had to study the files for his client Newport Inc, he would ask Akriti to "*get the first 10 of the blue files on the 5th rack, shelf number 3*". And if, after going through those 10 files, Mr. Bhalla could not find the required information and wanted to see the other files for the same client, he would call Akriti and ask her to "*get the next 5 blue files on the 5th rack, shelf number 3*". This was a waste of time for both Bhalla and Akriti. But as Akriti started gaining experience, he decided to give "less" information to her, and let her do most of the job herself. So he would give her brief instructions, and instead of "*get me the first 10 of the blue files on the 5th rack, shelf number 3*", he would just say "*give me all the files for Newport Inc*". He realized that this method was more efficient, and once all of files were on his desk, he could find the relevant information himself.

Basically, Bhalla moved from a fine-grained model to a coarse-grained one; towards a more "message" based system instead of a method-calling system (give me "this" based on "this, this and this" parameters). This coarse-grained model and message-based system is basically the essence of service orientation.

Service orientation means that the application's business logic is wrapped up and presented as a service to an outside client. This service is complete in itself. It doesn't need complex object relationships or **Component Oriented Middleware (COM)**-like middleware to render itself to its consumers. With the advent of web services, SOA architecture has become extremely easy to implement.

Service orientation was born out of this need for better change management, process alignment, and improved efficiency in automating complex and changing business rules. Object orientation focuses more on breaking the business model into an object model and interaction between different business objects according to business rules. It focuses more on how to best implement a particular business model as a domain model in an application.

As OOAD evolved, it became more and more involved with the actual implementation part of the architecture. But with time, the need for better integration and faster response time for business software was felt. It was hard for a new application to communicate with the existing legacy systems (old software), and cross-platform integration became complex and time consuming. A need for an easier solution, that is, an architecture that would solve these problems from a business point of view, and is also easy to implement, was felt. Thus, Service Oriented Architecture was born.

SOA helps businesses to manage changes in their applications better and faster and get a higher Return On Investments (ROI) by promoting the re-use of different application components.

Let us look at the following diagram, which depicts the usual communication between different components in an object-based software system:

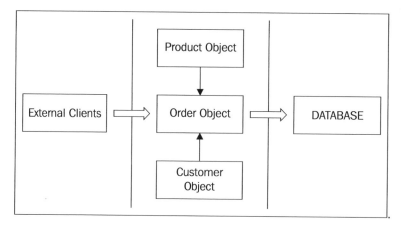

In traditional object-oriented systems, external clients (outside applications) need to understand the application's domain model in order to interact with it. The domain model was quite complex, and the external clients had to understand the fine-grained API, or use complex middleware technologies such as COM/COM+ to integrate applications.

With SOA, a service interface was built and the methods were exposed as coarse-grained units, performing individual database transactions to fetch/put data. And web services allowed easy portability and integration across platforms.

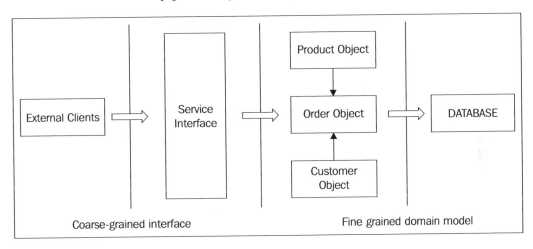

So we can abstract the conceptual fine-grained domain model by building an interface layer over it, which has relatively coarse-grained methods when compared to those in the model. These methods in turn interact with the domain model and provide an easy-to-use interface for external clients. Such coarse-grained methods can easily be implemented using XML web services.

XML Web Services and SOAP Messages

XML web services are software components used to communicate and share data between distributed systems. XML web services are simple to build and use, and can talk to disparate systems across networks.

We can use XML web services to create an SOA based framework. Using web services, we can create message-based systems, and implement web methods that are complete in themselves. This means that our web methods should not depend on or call other web methods, and should be independent entities in themselves, so that they can be called as a "message" by external clients. If the web methods depend on each other, then the system will become tightly-coupled, and break the basic principle of SOA, which is to keep components loosely coupled.

External clients should be able to talk to our system using messages, as shown here:

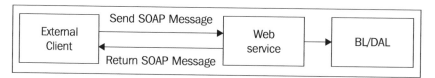

The above diagram depicts an XML web service using the Simple Object Access Protocol (SOAP) for exchanging data across the systems. SOAP is a lightweight XML-based protocol. SOAP can be used to serialize objects and data across HTTP using the XML format.

Behind the service interface, we can use our normal domain model. The main idea behind using web services is to make each part or module independent of the other parts or modules, in order to achieve a higher degree of loose coupling. We will use coarse-grained web services to achieve fewer calls, and wrap fine-grained business logic, exposing it as coarse-grained messages to the outside world.

Sample Project

Let's study a sample project using XML web services with VS 2008, and create a service interface for our Order Management System. We will perform the following:

1. Use the 5-tier solution we created in Chapter 4.

2. Create a service interface around it using XML web services in an SOA-like fashion.

3. Allow the GUI to talk to this interface instead of using the business layer directly.

 We can also use the sample code created in Chapter 5 using MVC. MVC and SOA complement each other, and one should not get confused with the question, "should I use MVC or SOA?" MVC has a purpose different from that of SOA, and can be used in any SOA implementation.

In this example, our main aim is to see how a service interface can provide another level of abstraction between the GUI and BL/DAL tiers, and enable our project to talk to multiple clients (or GUIs) using XML web services. Let's look at a simple example that illustrates how loose coupling can be implemented.

Building a Service Interface

Let us open the same 5-tier project that we created in Chapter 4. Add a new ASP. NET web services project to the solution, and name it NTier.Services:

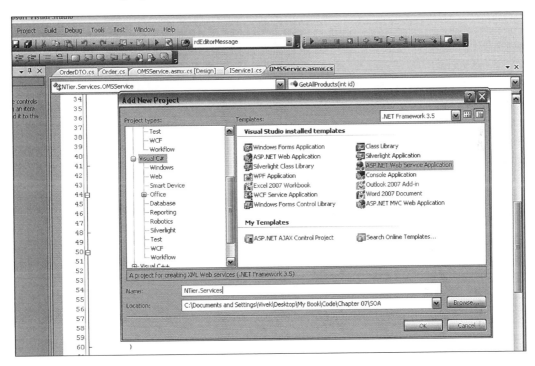

Now right-click on the new **NTier.Services** project, select **Add New Item**, and from that dialog box select the **Web Service** option. Name the file OMSService. asmx. The ASMX extension is used to denote web service files in the Microsoft .NET framework, and they are basically placeholders from where our main web service code runs. In an asmx.cs file, we can have multiple web methods (denoted by the [WebMethod] attribute before the method definition).

We will create a simple web method that returns a list of products in an XML SOAP format, in our newly-created OMSService.asmx.cs code file. Note that the VS and the .NET framework make it very easy for us to create and consume web services, as most of the SOAP formatting and other related work is handled by VS, letting us focus on the web methods. Here is how our FindAllCustomers method in the Business Layer looks (as seen in Chapter 4):

```
public Collection<Customer> FindAll(LoadStatus loadStatus,
        int start,int pageLength, out int noOfPages)
    {
        try
        {
        Collection<CustomerDTO> dtoList =
        CustomerDAL.GetAllCustomers(
        loadStatus,start, out noOfPages);
        foreach(CustomerDTO dto in dtoList)
            Customer customer = new Customer(dto);
            this.Add(customer);
        }
        return this;
    }
catch(Exception ex)
        {
        //handle exception
        throw;
    }
```

This returns a strongly-typed collection of Customer objects by calling the DAL method from CustomerDAL (for details of these methods, please refer to Chapter 4).

Now, we define a new web method in our OMSService.asmx.cs file called GetAllCustomers(), and call the BL method as follows:

```
/// <summary>
/// Get all customers
/// </summary>
/// <returns>An array of customer DTOs</returns>
[WebMethod]
public CustomerDTO[] GetAllCustomers()
{
    CustomerCollection customers = new CustomerCollection();
    CustomerDTO[] customerArray;
    //get all customers so set page length =-1 indicating
    full load
```

```
            int pageLength = -1;
            //start from 1st record
            int start = 1;
            int noOfPages;
            //call domain method
            Collection<Customer> customersList
            = customers.FindAll(LoadStatus.Loaded,1,pageLength,
             out noOfPages);
            customerArray = new CustomerDTO[customersList.Count];
            for(int i=0; i<customersList.Count; i++)
            {
                customerArray[i] = customersList[i].DTO;
            }
            return customerArray;
    }
```

The above web method returns a list of of all the customers from the database. The GetAllCustomers() method uses the domain method FindCustomers() and converts the strongly-typed collection of Customer objects returned into an array of CustomerDTOs. The highlights of this very simple method are:

- The method returns a list of data transfer objects instead of core domain objects. This helps us stop the domain model from being exposed to external clients and also helps us include loose coupling in our system.

- The web method uses the domain model internally to get a list of objects to be returned to the outside caller. So the interface layer abstracts the business layer by creating wrappers around it, and external clients (consuming our service interface) do not need to know anything about domain model internals, as long as they know which web methods to call and with what parameters.

- This web method can be used in any external client irrespective of the platform on which the client is running. This is possible because web services use the XML format which is generic across all platforms. So an application running on a JAVA platform can call our method and use it internally.

- This method has no arguments, but it is calling a domain method internally:

```
customers.FindAll(LoadStatus.Loaded,1,pageLength,
        out noOfPages);
```

  which takes `LoadStatus`, start page, `pageLength` and number of pages as arguments. We have specified `pageLength` as 1 so that we can get all of the records. This is a very simple example of how we can wrap fine-grained functionality with coarse-grained methods to be exposed to external clients. It is up to the consuming client to handle the returned data, and page it as per the client's own external logic. Our aim should be to simply return as much data as we can in one trip, and avoid making multiple trips across the network (which can be performance-intensive). Because we do not know what logic external clients might have in their own domain model, we have to keep our service interface as simple and generic as possible, and leave the data manipulation and logic to the clients themselves.

We know that DTOs are serializable (marked with the `serialize` attribute). But if we simply returned the generic list of DTOs, we would face two problems:

- We would need to serialize the generic list. This is an easy task and does not require complex coding.
- Only clients based on NET 2.0 or above would be able to use the web service, as generic objects are a .NET 2.0-only feature. So having a generic list in the method signature is not a good idea.

To avoid these two issues, we should always try for simple data types in web service method signatures. That is the reason we have used arrays in the above sample method.

Consuming Services

Now we will see how we can use this service in our web forms UI instead of using business objects directly. If you recall, in Chapter 4, our `showAll.aspx` form had displayed a list of all of the customers using the code shown here (taken from the `showAll.aspx.cs` code-behind file in Chapter 4, a 5-tier source code):

```
/// <summary>
/// Get and Show a list of all customers
/// </summary>
private void FillAllCustomers()
{
    CustomerCollection customers = new CustomerCollection();
    int noOfPages;
    int pageLength = -1;
    int start = 1;
```

```
rptCustomers.DataSource
= customers.FindAll(LoadStatus.Loaded, start,
-1, out noOfPages);
rptCustomers.DataBind();
}
```

Here, we are using the business object `CustomerCollection`, in the code-behind GUI class. Now we will see how we can consume this service without using the domain classes directly, but using the service interface layer instead.

First, we need to add a reference to the ASMX web services; right-click the **5Tier.Web** project in VS and select **Add Web Reference** (see the following screenshot):

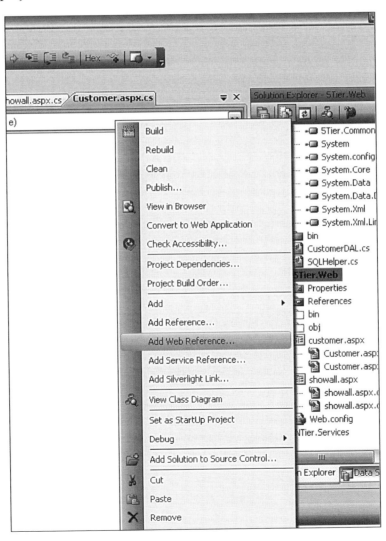

In the **Add Web Reference** dialog box that is displayed, we will select the **Web Services in this solution** option, as shown in the following screenshot:

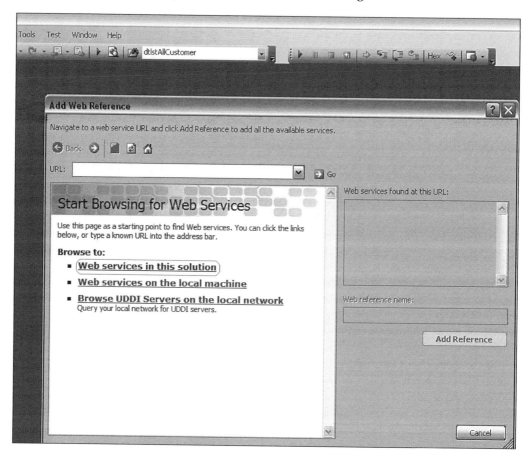

We selected this option because we knew that our web service project is inside our main solution file. In the forthcoming section, we will see how we can select and consume a web service from a different project by using other options shown in this dialog box.

After selecting the **Web services in this Solution** option, VS will display a list of services available for us to use, as shown below:

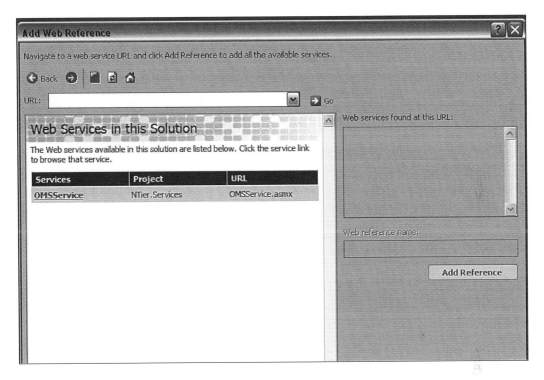

VS scanned our projects and found the `OMSservice.asmx` file that we created earlier in the `NTier.Services` project. When you click the **OMSService** in the dialog box, VS will show you a list of all of the web methods from that service, as shown below:

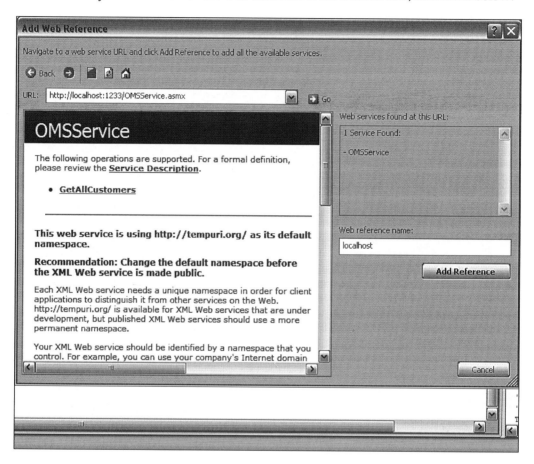

Since we only had the **GetAllCustomers** web method, VS has displayed that in the list. You can give the web reference any name you want (the default is **localhost**) and then click the **Add Reference** button. VS will then add a web reference to this service in your web UI project. You will notice that while adding the web reference VS has automatically generated a bunch of files as shown below (you need to select the **Show hidden Files** option at the top of the **Solution Explorer** in VS to see these files):

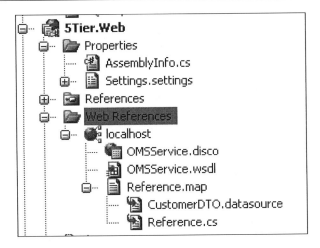

This shows that VS has completed all of the necessary work to make sure that our web services can be used in this UI project.

Next, open the `showall.aspx.cs` file; we will change the code to display a list of customers who can use the web service interface. as follows:

```
/// <summary>
/// Get and Show a list of all customers
/// </summary>
private void FillAllCustomers()
        {
            localhost.OMSService service =
            new NTier.Web.localhost.OMSService();
            CustomerDTO[] customers = service.GetAllCustomers();
            rptCustomers.DataSource = customers;
            rptCustomers.DataBind();
        }
```

In the above method, we create a new instance of our OMSService and call it as a service. Then we call the GetAllCustomers web method that returns an array of customer data transfer objects. We then bind these DTOs to the repeater. Note that in this code, we did not use any object in the domain model directly (as was done in the same code in Chapter 4). We used only the service interface and the data transfer object that belongs to the NTier.Common project, which is common to all the projects.

Now let us understand how we can use this service in an external project. First, we need to host this web service on a server so that it can be discovered and referenced by external programs. For this, simply create a virtual directory in your local web server (you can name it **OMSService**) and then publish the NTier.Service project to that virtual directory. We will create a simple console application using Visual Studio (VS) and then call this web service to display a list of customers. Here are the steps:

1. Create a new VS solution and select **Add New Project**.
2. Select **Console Application** and name it **Service Consumer**.
3. Right-click on the newly-added project in VS and select **Add Reference**.
4. Add a reference to the **5Tier.Common** project. This is needed because we need to use the CustomerDTO class, which is being returned by our service. If we don't want to use the 5Tier.Common project, then we can create our own DTO class with the same name and having the same properties.
5. Right-click the project again and select the **Add Service Reference** option.
6. In the dialog box that is displayed, type the address of the OMS web service, which you hosted on your local server. The address should look something like this: http://localhost/OMSService/OMSService.asmx. Here is a screenshot of how the dialog box will look:

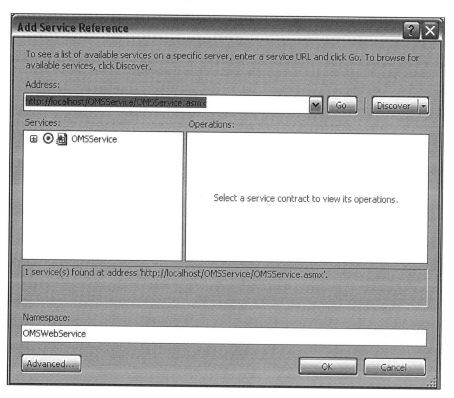

7. In the **Namespace** field, type **OMSWebService** and click the **OK** button.

8. The service reference will be added to the console application project and VS will auto-generate the files shown below (you need to select the **Show hidden Files** option at the top of the **Solution Explorer** in VS to see these files):

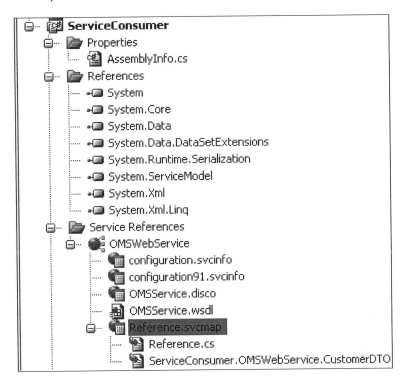

9. Now, open the `Program.cs` file, and include the following lines to show a list of customers by consuming the `OMSservice`:

```
static void Main(string[] args)
        {
            OMSWebService.OMSServiceSoapClient client =
            new ServiceConsumer.OMSWebService.
                    OMSServiceSoapClient();
            CustomerDTO[] customers = client.GetAllCustomers();
            foreach (CustomerDTO customer in customers)
            {
                Console.WriteLine(customer.Name);
            }
        }
```

Here we are calling the `GetAllCustomers` method and showing the names of all of the customers.

The above two simple examples show us how the web service interface is managing fine-grained object orientation in a web method and exposing simple coarse-grained methods. Therefore, a service method is a complete independent entity in itself, performing complete end-to-end operations without depending on other service methods.

Windows Communication Foundation

Windows Communication Foundation, known as WCF for short, is a wrapper around the .NET 2.0 framework, and is designed to facilitate the use of SOA for .NET applications in a simple and flexible way.

But why is WCF needed? The ASMX web services we used in the previous sections were the best way to implement a cross-platform SOA-based architecture. But when we need to implement ASMX services to interact with other platforms such as J2EE (Java Enterprise Edition, a platform for developing applications using the Java language), we will most probably need to use a mixture of technologies, such as ASMX web services along with **Web Service Enhancements (WSE)**.

WSE is an implementation of the web services architecture for developers creating web services using ASP.NET and Microsoft .NET Framework client applications. WSE was introduced to help create scalable web services, with a special focus on security. Dealing with cross-platform security, as in, say, a .NET service interacting with a J2EE based client, is quite complex, requiring the consideration of two completely separate security domains. To solve such issues, WSE was released by Microsoft. WSE with ASMX web services solved the integration issues with .NET and J2EE.

With WCF, Microsoft bundled everything together by implementing interoperable web services complete with cross-platform security, reliability, transactions, and other services. Now, there is no need to use remoting; WCF is the way to go. WCF can work with SOAP, RSS, or any other custom message format, simply by extending it. Also, WCF carries considerable performance gains when compared to standard ASMX web services.

Remoting is a system for Microsoft .NET platform that enables interprocess communication in a homogenous environment. With the help of remoting, we can communicate between two processes running on different machines (or different application domains) in a network (but having the same OS). Because remoting uses binary serialization, it is much faster than using web services. However, we cannot use remoting in a heterogeneous environment (say, where an ASP.NET web application is talking to a J2EE application) using a .NET specific API, as other systems, such as J2EE, cannot understand it. Also, the use of remoting when we want to talk to processes outside of the LAN (say, when communicating using WAN or Internet) can be troublesome, as it cannot bypass a firewall until specific access is given to the service. Using web services is preferred in such cases.

In this section, we will understand how to use WCF instead of ASMX services. We will not be going into detail as this chapter is more focused on the use of WCF for SOA, and is not intended to serve as a primer to WCF.

A WCF service is composed of three main components:

- **A WCF service class:** This contains the actual implementation of the methods. This class is similar in purpose to the class defined in the ASMX.CS code file earlier. This class will hold the code logic for the WCF Service.

- **Host Environment:** Any parent process that can host the service, such as a console application, or an IIS or Windows application.

- **Service Endpoints:** These are the communication endpoints of the service. Each service can have a collection of endpoints. Each end point is a combination of address, binding, and contract. End points can be created through code as well as through the configuration class. These end points act as the "gateways" for communicating with the outside world.

WCF treats data exchange between the applications more like a message exchange, rather than treating it is as a simple procedure call (which is how default ASMX web services are treated using web methods).

Sample Project using WCF

Let us understand WCF through a sample project. We will modify the project we started above to use WCF services instead of ASMX services. Open the same solution in which we created the previous OMSService and add a new WCF service file named OMSWCFService.svc to the NTier.Services project.

You will notice that VS automatically creates IOMSWCFService.cs and adds the necessary service registration information in the web.config file.

```
namespace NTier.Services
{
    [ServiceContract]
    public interface IOMSWCFService
    {
        [OperationContract]
        void DoWork();
    }
}
```

This file contains the definition of the interface that will be used as a service contract.

> If you want, you can define the implementation class immediately, without defining the interface. In this case you would need to use the ServiceContract and OperationContract attributes directly in the implementation class.

Now, we need to define the methods that we want to expose in our implementation class. Let us put the method signature of the GetAllProducts() method here:

```
using NTier.Business;
using NTier.Common.DTO;
namespace NTier.Services
{
    [ServiceContract]
    public interface IOMSWCFService
    {
        [OperationContract]
        ProductDTO[] GetAllProducts(int);
    }//end interface
}//end class
```

The implementation class will look like this:

```
namespace NTier.Services
{
    // NOTE: If you change the class name "OMSWCFService" here, you
must also update the reference to "OMSWCFService" in Web.config.
    public class OMSWCFService : IOMSWCFService
    {
        /// <summary>
        /// Get all products
```

```
///   </summary>
///   <param name="id"></param>
///   <returns></returns>
public ProductDTO[] GetAllProducts(int id)
{
    Product p = new Product();
    ProductDTO[] pa;
    //return all products
    p.GetAllProducts();
    pa = new ProductDTO[p.ProductList.Count];
    return pa;
}
    }//end class
}//end namespace
```

Note that we don't need to use the `[WebMethod]` identifier here as it was used in ASMX services. Using WCF instead of ASMX services is recommended because WCF is a more complete and easy-to-use platform when compared to simple ASMX web services. Hence, WCF helps us write better services that are more useful in an SOA environment.

Summary

Enabling SOA in your .NET applications is not a difficult task. SOA implementations use object-oriented techniques internally, but provide a simple, platform-independent coarse-grained interface to be used by any client, independent of the technology used. Because XML is an open standard, using SOA guarantees that your system can talk to any other system, be it built in PHP, JAVA or any other platform.

SOA architecture should not be used everywhere without proper forethought. There is no need for SOA architecture when we are sure that the application is small and limited in scope as well as potential growth.

ASMX web services were one of the best ways to implement SOA-based architectures. But, Microsoft's WCF framework works best when one has to integrate all of the service-oriented techniques into one framework, as it is easy to use and involves less complexity. Considering the richness of WCF over ASMX, it is suggested that all services should be implemented in WCF only.

All of these topics are very important to understand, and will help us make the right choices when selecting an architectural platform for our web applications. By leveraging this knowledge and experience, we can develop scalable and robust solutions that are flexible enough to cater for future needs.

8
Database Design

In the first two chapters, we learnt that we could divide our whole application into the following tiers:

- **Presentation Layer**: This is the client browser.
- **The UI layer**: An ASP.NET website having ASPX/ASCX web pages.
- **Business Logic Layer (BLL)**: This contains the business logic code.
- **Data Access Layer (DAL)**: This contains the data access code that talks to the data layer.
- **Common Tier**: This is just a class library that contains the Data Transfer Objects, or DTOs, used to pass data between the tiers. This tier also contains utility or helper methods that are common to all of the tiers.
- **Data Layer (DL)**: This is the physical database, such as the MS SQL Server; this can include text files or XML Files.

For the sake of convenience, let us revisit the diagram from Chapter 4 to see how all these tiers were interacting in a 5-tier system:

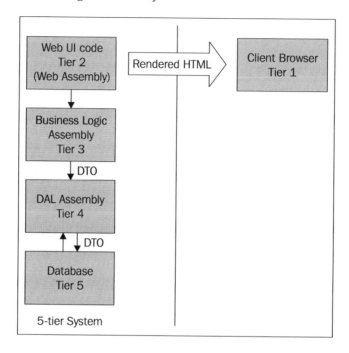

So far, we have focused on the UI, the BLL and the DAL layers, understanding the different application architectural approaches as well as different design and implementation methods that can be used to make the overall architecture more scalable and robust. But we really did not focus on how the actual database or the **Data Layer (DL)** can play an important role in making our application architecture better. This chapter is exclusively dedicated to modeling as well as designing our data layer.

In this chapter, we will try to understand:

- The importance of a well designed database
- Database Architecture and Design
- The Logical Data Model
- The Physical Data Model
- Normalization
- What Data Integrity is
- Using MS Visio to create a data model

The Importance of a Database

In today's information age, data is very valuable, and it is important to manage data properly. Data management can comprise of multiple steps such as:

- **Persisting data**: Data persistence means storing information properly so that it can be retrieved efficiently later on.

- **Organizing data**: Using proper data structures to store data so that disk space is utilized efficiently.

- **Manipulating data**: The data stored should be able to support `Create`, `Read`, `Update` and `Delete` (known as `CRUD` operations).

- **Searching data**: Making sure that data searches are performance-efficient and comprehensive.

- **Securing data**: Data is very valuable from a business standpoint. Proper security measures should be in place to make sure that data security is not compromised.

To achieve these goals, it is very important to select the correct data store, which is also called a database. The proper choice of a database depends on the application's actual requirements.

Selecting the Right Database

Most commercial applications today rely on some sort of external database for persistence. The most common methods to store data are:

- Text files
- XML files
- Relational databases
- Any other proprietary format

Text files are common for very small projects where we do not need to store complex data structures and there are no concurrency issues caused by the data being updated by multiple users. Adding the ability for users to simultaneously add or modify data in text files will take a lot of effort, and for such scenarios, it is recommended that you use a **Relational Database Management System (RDBMS)**.

But if your application doesn't need to store much data, then there is no need to go for an RDBMS. We can simply use the text files for the rarely-used data. Some examples of such applications can be:

- File encryption utilities that simply encrypt data in memory and then decrypt it as required. These files might need to store the encryption key in some text (or custom file) format.
- Other simple desktop based programs such as a calculator, calendar, and so on.
- Simple websites that display static information (such as company information) and do not store any data.

XML files are a better alternative to text files as they are generic and can be processed by multiple systems. XML files are also easy to access programmatically as there are a lot of in-built libraries in the .NET framework that can handle XML files. XML files can also handle large amounts of data efficiently, and use XPath as a query language to fetch data. XPath is a simple language that can be used to select nodes within any XML document. XML can be a good choice for an application such as a blogging platform. Storing information such as blog entries in XML format is convenient for producing **RSS (Really Simple Syndication)** feeds.

RDBMS is one of the best and most commonly used database formats today. Most of the commercial RDBMSes, such as SQL Server, Oracle, and so on provide a lot of advanced functionality so that the developer does not need to bother about the standard data management issues. RDBMS is the best choice for most commercial applications that need flexible data storage as well as efficient data retrieval and processing.

When selecting between XML and RDBMS, we need to consider the following points:

- XML data can be easily distributed and understood by different systems since it is a standard markup language supported by wide variety of diverse platforms. Transferring RDBMS is not that easy, as each RDBMS typically has its own proprietary format.
- An RDBMS has a lot of built-in tools for manipulating and querying data easily, whereas XML lacks such tools. Moreover, one has to create or buy custom tools for XML files in order to be able to manipulate data as easily as a commercial RDBMS can do. So it is obvious that an RDBMS is more than just a data file; it is an advanced program that provides a rich interface to handle data, whereas XML is just a simple file that has the data stored in a predefined format.
- Querying XML data (using XPath and XQuery) is more complex than using **Structure Query Language (SQL)** statements, which are supported by all major RDBMSes. So if your application queries a lot of data it would be better to use an RDBMS.

- For large enterprise applications, it is recommended that you use an RDBMS considering the large amount of data throughout involved.

Although many applications may use text files, XML files, or their own custom storage engines, in this chapter we will focus on the architectural aspect of designing and using a relational database for a web application.

Database Architecture and Design

Database design can also be considered as a part of the architecture of the application that uses an external database to persist data. A thoughtfully-designed database that is optimally normalized (normalization is a concept that we will learn later in this chapter) complements the system's architecture. In previous chapters, we learnt that each application demands its own unique application architecture. The same goes for database design too, where we design the schema to suit an application's unique requirements. What worked in one application's database design might not work in another.

Before going ahead with the actual database architecture and design, we need to create a plan for the database.

Database Plan

Creating a database plan is the first step in creating a database. The objective of the plan is to list the core requirements for the database as well as the scope of the database being designed. This plan will be useful in simplifying the process and mitigating any risks involved with the actual implementation of the database.

Because every application's data requirements are unique we need different plans to suit individual scenarios. Some applications might have multiple users accessing data, and this number may grow over time. Some applications might have few users, but the amount of data could be huge, and the application may have complex rules controlling that data. A proper database plan will address a project's requirements and will also serve as a functional specification for the database after it has been implemented. Therefore, the planning process will vary according to the nature and complexity of the project.

The following are the core steps in creating a plan for your database:

- Understanding the project's specific requirements
- Listing the major entities
- Indentifying the relationships between these entities

- Identifying the relationships between objects
- Addressing the scope of the application in terms of size, complexity and future scalability

Based on the project requirements, we have to create a model of the database. This model can also be called the design of the database. On a broader level, database design has two parts—logical design and physical design.

Logical Design

Logical design refers to establishing the relationship between the different system entities. For example, an employee can have multiple roles. So using a logical design, we can create relationships between the Employee entity and the Role entity.

Most projects start with the identification of the major entities in the system, and then progress to identifying relationships between these entities. Entity Relationship diagrams, or ER diagrams, which we learnt about in Chapter 3, are perfect for depicting such relationships. Once an ER diagram (which will also be the logical model of the database) has been defined, we can work on the object model design, called the **domain model**. In the domain model, we define different system entities (or objects), and define the relationships between them (such as association, aggregation, and so on). We have already created a domain model for our Order Management System (OMS) in Chapter 3.

In Chapter 3, we created a domain model and created our classes based on the domain model. This is known as Domain-Driven Design. But some projects may be heavily data-centric, with little or no business logic. Then the domain classes would not have much behavior in them. Such classes would then merely act as data containers. So in these cases, we can go for a Data-Driven approach, where we bypass the creation of a Domain model and start directly with the database entities and code using those classes. The Domain-Driven approach may take more time than the Data-Driven design, but is recommended because it helps in the long-term maintenance of the project code base by keeping the code more organized and flexible.

Once we have created the first drafts of both the ER diagram and the domain model, we evolve them in parallel by making changes in one and reflecting these updates in the other. It is not common to completely finalize an ER diagram and only then work on a domain model.

An important point to be noted here is that an object model entity is different from a data model entity. For example, both `Employee` and `Manager` are different entities in the Object Model, but they can be persisted in the same physical data table. Hence the data model entity would be the same for both the `Employee` and the `Manager`. A logical data model is independent of the database. So the same logical model can be used to design a physical model for Oracle, or MS SQL Server, or any other database.

An Example of a Logical Model

Let us revisit the ER diagram that we created for our Order Management System in Chapter 3.

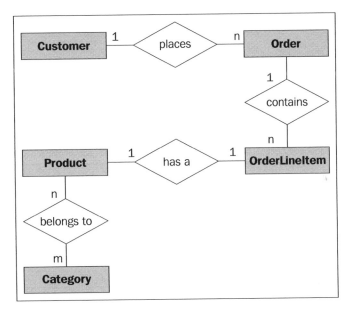

Although we have not shown any attributes of the entities here, an ER diagram can have attributes for each entity listed in the diagram. But I usually refer to the ER diagram for understanding entity relationships from a high level (without getting into the details of the attributes involved), and use the logical data model for a more complete picture of the database. The ER diagram here is basically a foundation for the logical data model for our database. Using an ER diagram, we can quickly see how different entities are related to each other, and this will help us in creating the right relationships in the Relational Database Management System. Let us create a logical data model for our database using the same ER diagram:

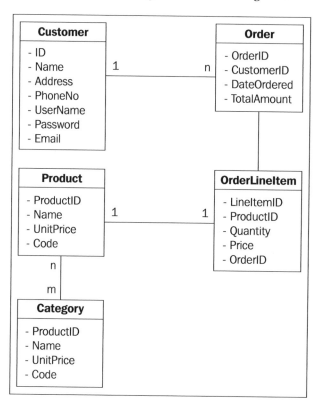

The above logical model has attributes and also depicts the relationships between the different entities, giving us a "plan" of the actual database that should be developed. It is very important to make sure that the logical data model is developed with a detailed understanding of the system, as this forms the foundation on which the final database will be developed. Changes to the logical data model should be avoided during the later stages of application development as they can be costly in terms of both time and money.

The Need for a Logical Data Model

A logical model is very helpful for the following reasons:

- **It helps in understanding project requirements**: A logical data model translates business requirements into simple entity relationship models, making it easy to identify and understand the business logic. Sometimes business requirements can be complex, making it difficult for the developer to understand a system's internal logic. Using a logical data model helps to create a visual representation of the system, from a high level.

- **It helps in creating the actual database**: The logical data model is the blueprint of the actual physical database that needs to be created for the application. Most beginner developers start creating physical tables in the database while starting to work on a project, which can lead to problems, as it might not be possible to foresee all of the physical tables and the relationships between them right at the start of the project. A logical data model helps in mitigating risks by laying out the entity relationships and attributes before the actual physical data modeling starts.

- **It is database independent**: The same logical data model can be used for different databases, as a logical model is independent of the physical database. This saves time when developing applications targeting multiple databases, which helps to reduce development time and cost.

The Domain Model Versus the Logical Data Model

Many developers are unclear of the difference between the domain model and the logical data model, sometimes mistaking one with the other. Even though a logical model might look similar to a domain model in terms of depicting primary entities of a system, there are fundamental differences between the two. A logical data model is more focused on the structure of the data in the entities and on the relationships between different entities, whereas a domain model is focused on encapsulating the entities from an object-oriented perspective. So a logical data model is purely relational in nature, but an object domain model is richer, depicting inheritance, associations, aggregations, and so on, between the different entities involved.

In our object model, there will be some entities that will be the same as in the logical data model, whereas some might not be present in the logical data model at all. For example, if we create a parent class for a `Customer` called `Person`, then in the object model, the entities would look like this:

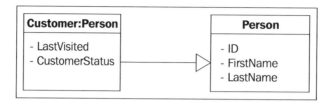

Here, the `Customer` class inherits the `Person` class, and both are different kinds of objects in the domain model. Even though we can say `Customer` is a type of `Person`, but not every `Person` is a `Customer`. So both of these entities need to be depicted separately in the domain model.

But in the logical data model, we cannot depict inheritance or any other object-oriented feature. In this case, both the `Person` and the `Customer` classes can be persisted in the same table in the database. So there would be a single entity for both of these in the logical data model as shown here:

How, then, do we identify Persons from Customers? One simple way is to add a Boolean attribute: `IsCustomer`. For all `Person` objects who are Customers, this attribute would be true. This is one simple example to show that the relational data model is very different from an object-oriented domain model.

Physical Data Model

Once we have defined the logical data model, we can then create a physical data model for our application. A logical model is closer to the business model whereas a physical model actually mirrors the actual database. In short, the physical data model is the logical data model with:

- Table names for all of logical entities. These table names would be the same as the actual table names in the database.

- Physical data types and sizes for all of the attributes. In the physical model, we will supply the data types of the entity attributes, such as `varchar`, `int`, `float`, and so on, along with the data type size. Because each database has its own unique set of physical data types, the physical model is dependent upon the type of database being used.

- Mapping tables or cross tables are used for storing many-to-many relationships within entities. A logical data model might not include mapping tables, but might simply depict such many-to-many relationship between entity A and B using m:n notation. But in a database, such relations need to be stored in another table, which we can refer to as cross or mapping table. Such tables are depicted in the physical data model (we will see one such example soon).

- Primary keys, foreign keys, indexes, and so on.

 A primary key is an attribute which uniquely identifies a record in a table. If a primary key contains two or more attributes, it is called as a Composite Key.

A physical design represents the complete model of the database. It is the schema of the database being designed. The actual selection of the data types is dependent on the database system being used. We can do this either by creating or modifying the tables in the database or by using a modeling tool such as Microsoft Visio. Such tools are immensely useful for creating and managing data models, as one can generate database schema as well as create and share database diagrams based on different database providers.

While working on the physical model, we need to make sure that we use the right data types. Also, we need to be consistent with the data types. For example, all unique identifier columns (like the primary keys) should be of one data type. If we decide to support localized data, then we should use `nvarchar` instead of `varchar`. A proper selection of data types would ensure that our data model is scalable as well as flexible, in order to incorporate future changes.

Data Integrity

Referential integrity means that all of the primary and foreign keys in a database are valid, and no invalid links exist between the various tables that make up the system. Let's understand this with a simple example. Assume we have a `Customer` table, with a primary key of `CustomerID` and other related fields such as `First Name`, `Last name`, and so on.

Now we enter our first customer, and set the `CustomerID` to 1. Then we enter a second customer and set the new row's `CustomerID` to 2. Now if we update this second row, and change its `CustomerID` to 1, then the data integrity of our database system would be compromised, as we will have multiple customers with the same `CustomerID`.

To avoid such issues, we can use the Identity feature of SQL Server to auto-increment the primary key values. We will learn more about using identities later in this section.

Also, data integrity has to be maintained when using foreign keys. Foreign keys help in creating relationships between the two tables, where we create a reference by using the primary key of one table as a foreign key in the other. So if the row being referenced in the primary table is deleted, we need to make sure that we delete all references to that primary key from any related tables; otherwise the links would be left "hanging", or pointing to nothing.

We can maintain referential integrity by creating relationships in SQL Server. We will see an example of this later in this section.

Normalization

Normalization is a very important step towards creating a functional and efficient database model. Normalization is a process whereby we remove redundant data from tables and save valuable disk space by minimizing duplication of data. In this book we will not go into the basic process of normalization and the different normal forms, but will have a look at how under-normalization and over-normalization can cause issues and should be avoided.

To understand normalization in depth, refer to this book:

C. J. Date (1999), *An Introduction to Database Systems (8th edition)*. Addison-Wesley Longman. ISBN 0-321-19784-4.

Let us understand under normalization first. Assume that we are developing a simple Library Management System. We identify Book as the first entity, and start listing its different fields:

- `Book ID`
- `Title`
- `ISBN`
- `AuthorName`
- `PublisherName`

Now assume that we have created a Book table in the database with these fields, and entered a list of books:

BookID	Title	ISBN	AuthorName	AuthorAddress	PublisherName
1	Advanced C# 3.5	555-66	James Hetfield	33, 4th Street, CA	MTL Pvt Ltd
2	ASP.NET 3.5	4343-443	Kirk Hammet	56, Dersy Drive, NC	MTL Pvt Ltd
3	AJAX Simplified	334-34341	James Hetfield	33, 4th Street, CA	MTL Pvt Ltd
4	ADO.NET Internals	323-234	James Hetfield	33, 4th Street, CA	NPS Pvt Ltd

Now, there are some problems with this design, as listed below:

- If we want to have 100 rows of books written by the author James Hetfield, we will need to repeat `AuthorName` and `AuthorAddress` 100 times (once for each row), wasting valuable disk space and creating redundant data.

- If we want to retrieve a list of authors from the table above using an SQL query, we will need to make sure that we filter our repeated names.

- If we delete a book, the author would be deleted too, along with the publisher. Authors and Publishers are not dependent on the Books, so having the above design is a major drawback.

- If we need to update a publisher or an author, we have to update each row for every book published by that publisher or written by that author, which not only degrades performance but is also a cumbersome task.

To fix these issues, we need to normalize the data model and put the author and publisher details in separate individual tables. So instead of one Book table, we will have three tables:

- Book
- Author
- Publisher

This way, we will remove the dependency of Books on Authors and Publishers.

Book	Author	Publisher
- BookID	- AuthorID	- PublisherID
- Title	- FirstName	- Name
- ISBN	- LastName	- Company
- AuthorID		
- PublisherID		

So now we have three normalized tables, and instead of repeating the authors in the Books table, we are now referencing authors from the Author table using `AuthorID` as a foreign key in the Book table.

When we normalize a table, we basically break it up into different tables. This means increased complexity when querying data as we now need to use multiple tables instead of a single table. We need to have a balance between normalization and performance of the queries (joins). For example, we know that many customers could have a common last name, but we cannot create another table for `LastName`. So sometimes we may want to 'denormalize' data for better performance.

Moreover, we don't need to normalize when archiving data. So data stored in archived tables (historical data) should be denormalized so that queries can run faster and be performance-efficient.

Data Modeling using MS Visio

Let us create a physical data model for our Order Management System from the logical data model we developed in this chapter. Although we will create a physical data model targeting Microsoft SQL Server 2005, you can use the same method to target any database you want.

There are many tools, which allow us to create physical data models. Here are some of them:

- Microsoft Visio, from Microsoft
- ERWin Data Modeler, from Computer Associates
- Toad Data Modeler, from Quest.com

For our example, we will use Microsoft Visio. You can download a 60-day trial version of MS Visio from this link:

```
http://office.microsoft.com/en-us/visio/default.aspx
```

After you have downloaded and installed MS Visio, open it by going to **Start | Program Files | Microsoft Office | Microsoft Visio Professional**. Then select **File | New | Database | Database Model Diagram**, as shown in the following screenshot:

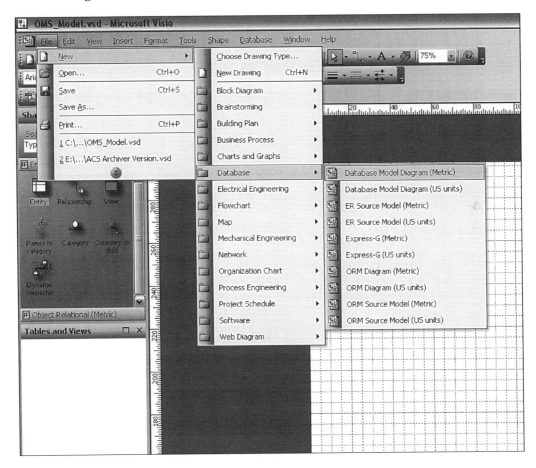

Once you have selected a database model diagram save it as: `OMS_Model.vsd`. Next, since we are targeting MS SQL Server, we will set the data model specific to MS SQL Server drivers. Here are the steps:

1. Select the **Database** menu on the top menu bar.

2. Select **Options | Drivers** from the drop-down menu, as shown in the following screenshot:

3. Select **Microsoft SQL Server** from the Database Drivers window and click **OK**, as shown in the following screenshot:

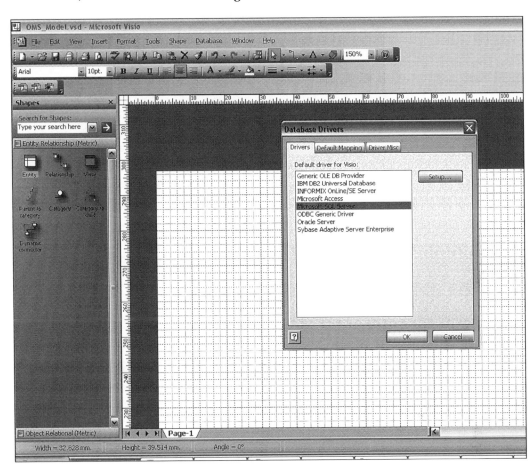

Now we will create the database tables based on the logical data model we created earlier. On the left side, you will see the **Shapes** pane, as shown below:

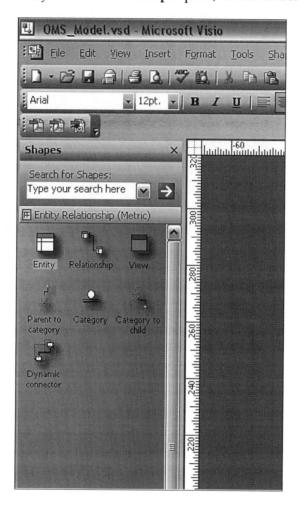

 If the Shapes pane is not visible, go to the top menu, select **View** and then select **Shapes** from the sub-menu.

The **Shapes** window has the most common shapes used to represent the entities we will use in our physical data model. We will only use the basic shapes, such as the **Entity** shape to represent an actual table in the database, and the **Relationship** shape to create relationships between the two entities.

Creating Physical Tables

Now drag-and-drop a new shape onto the modeling page and name it
OMS_Customer. To name it, you need to double-click on the shape so that
Database Properties box opens up below the drawing area, and then enter the
physical definition name in the **Definition** category of the **Database Properties**
window, as shown here:

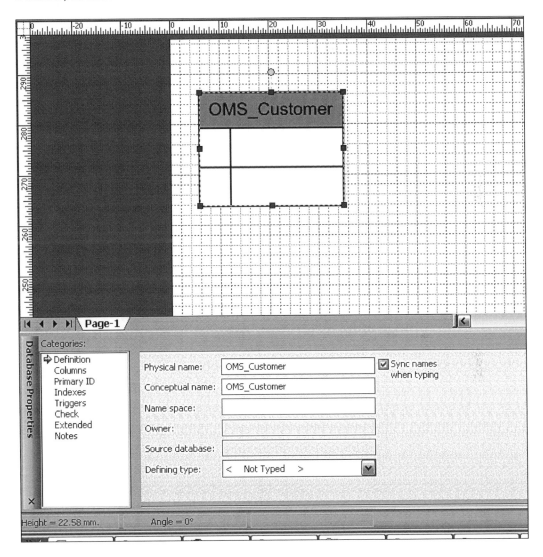

Next, we will add columns (fields) to this table, based on the logical model. In the same **Database Properties** window, select the **Columns** category, and add the columns shown below:

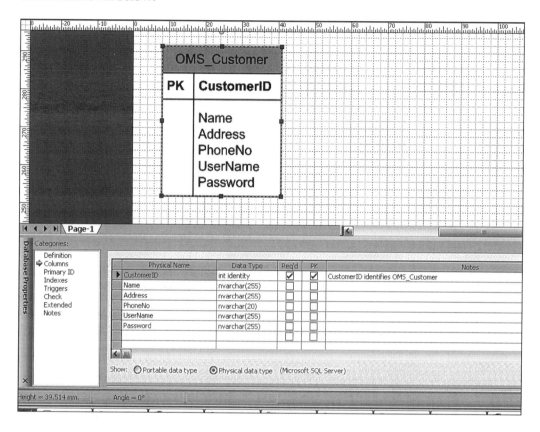

Note how the **CustomerID** column has been marked as a primary key by selecting the **PK** checkbox. Visio will highlight all of the primary keys in bold in the entity table in the drawing area. We can also identify which fields are required, and which can be null using the **Req'd** checkbox. We can also specify the physical data type of the columns. This will be useful when we will use MS Visio to generate a database creation script once our physical model is finalized.

After adding all of the columns, we want to set the **CustomerID** column as an identity in our SQL Server database. An identity is an SQL Server database-specific feature where the database itself increments and sets the value of the primary key (field) and in doing so makes sure that each value in the table is unique. We can set a column as an identity by following these steps:

1. Select the column in the **Database Properties** window.

2. Click the **Edit** button on the right most side.

3. In the dialog box that is displayed, click on the **Data Type** tab.

4. Make sure that **Show physical data type** option button (at the bottom) is checked.

5. Click on the **Edit** tab.

6. In the **Microsoft SQL Server Data Type** dialog box that is displayed, select the **Identity** checkbox. Then click the **OK** button.

Here is a screenshot showing the culmination of these steps, before the **OK** button is clicked.

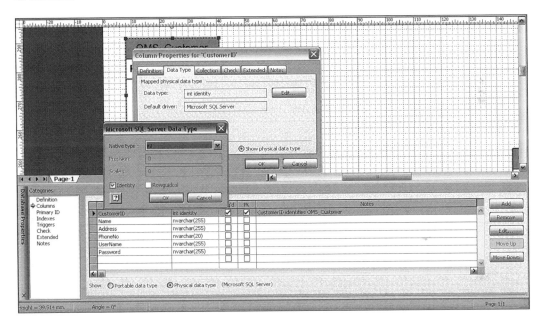

Similarly, create tables for the other entities by dragging and dropping entity shapes onto the drawing area. After adding the attributes and the physical data types, here is how the data model should look:

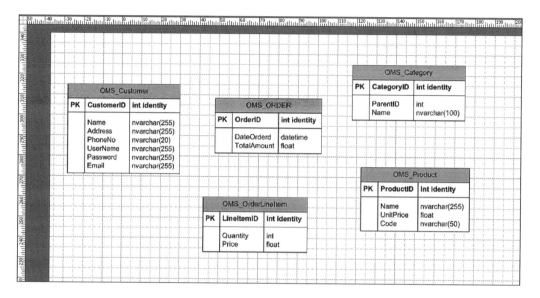

In the above diagram, we have added all of the entities that we created in the logical model, along with their physical data types. The only missing part is the relationships between the entities. So let us now see how we can define different types of relationships between the entities we created, using Visio.

Creating Relationships

To create a 1:n relationship (refer our earlier ER diagram for an explanation about 1:n relationships) between OMS_Customer and OMS_Order table, we need to follow these simple steps:

1. Drag and drop a **Relationship** connector from the **Shapes** pane onto the drawing area.

2. You will notice that the relationship connector has an arrow head at one end. Drag the arrow and drop it inside the OMS_Customer table.

3. Drag the other end of the **Relationship** connector and drop it inside the OMS_Order table.

4. Visio will automatically create a relationship between the Customer and Order tables by including CustomerID as a foreign key (FK) in the Order table.

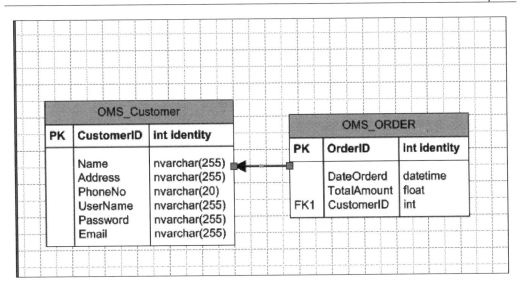

When creating a relationship, always remember that the arrow should point from the dependent entity to the parent entity. In the above case, Order is dependent on Customer, so we have the relationship diagram from the Order table to the Customer table.

To create a many-to-many (m:n) relationship, we need to create a separate table that can hold such a relationship. Such tables are sometimes referred to as mapping tables or cross tables.

In our ER diagram, there is a many-to-many relationship between the Product and Category entities. Each product can belong to multiple categories, so we cannot put CategoryID in the Product table as an Foreign Key (FK) because then we will be restricting each Product row to have only one Category (which would be a one-to-many relationship). Similarly, each Category can have multiple products listed under it, so we cannot add ProductID as a foreign key in the Category table, because then we will have a one-to-many relationship between Category and Products. So to have a many-to-many relationship, we need to create a new table which will contain only the ProductID and CategoryID columns, so that we can add multiple combinations of Product-Category to it. We will do this by creating a table named: OMS_XProductCategory. We can use any naming convention here but it is better to follow a certain standard and stick to it.

Here we have used "x" to signify that this table is a "cross" table. Once we have created the table, we will drag and drop two relationship connectors onto our drawing and add relationships from both of the OMS_Product and OMS_Category tables to the OMS_XProductCategory table as shown here:

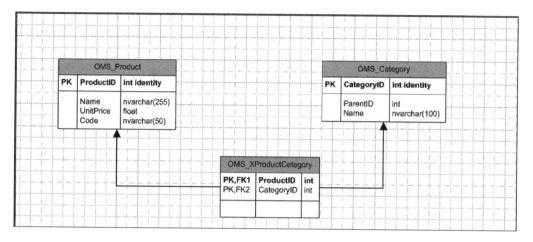

After adding the ProductId and CategoryID, we mark them as required (by checking **Req'd** in the **Database Properties** box) and set them both as the Primary Key (PK), making the combination of CategoryID and ProductID a **Composite key** in the OMS_XProductCategory table.

Here is the final physical data model, after adding all of the relationships and data types:

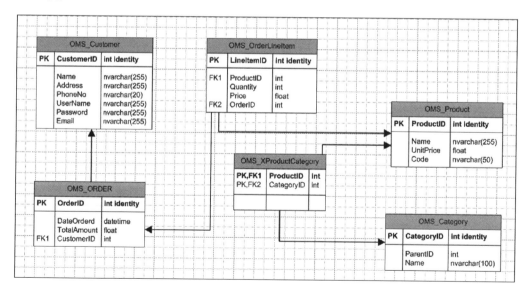

You can also generate a **Database Definition Language (DDL)** script file using Visio. This script can be run in the actual SQL Server database to create the complete database schema.

To create the DDL script, go to the **Database** menu on the top menu, and select **Generate Wizard** option. The following screen is displayed:

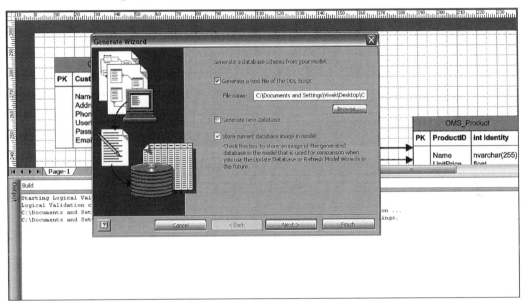

Specify the name and location to where you want to save the generated DDL script file, click **OK**, then click the **Next** button, and then name the Database **OMS**. Now, select **Next** and click **Finish**. You can then run the generated DLL file on the SQL Server to create the physical database.

Summary

In this chapter, we focused on the design aspects of creating and maintaining a database. We also learnt that a relational model does not understand inheritance, interfaces or polymorphism, some common attributes of object-oriented development. Hence, we need to map the object model to the relational data model appropriately so that we can save the domain objects in an efficient way. The logical data model helps us achieve this goal.

It is very important to understand and learn the differences between the logical and physical data models so that we have a clear understanding of the application. Equally important is the normalization of the database; both over- and under- normalized databases should be avoided. Also, design tools like MS Visio help us to create data models for our database including relationships and DDL scripts, which cut down on development time besides making the project more "understandable" with rich diagrams of the data model. So such tools are very important for developers to learn and use them as development aide while working on commercial projects.

9
Localization

You may be wondering why a chapter on localization would be included in a book on ASP.NET architecture and design. As explained earlier, the primary goal of this book is to make the developer familiar with all of the major aspects—from architecture and design to implementation—so that he or she can develop and design medium to large-scale web applications. There are many tasks that go into the making of a scalable multilingual ASP.NET web application. Making sure that the application is capable of supporting different cultures and locales is one of them.

The fact is that most web applications do not focus only on users belonging to a specific region but cater to users spread across various countries and continents. It makes more business sense to launch applications in multiple countries and target users around the world. For this to be possible, we have to make sure that our application is usable by people from different countries and cultures, as not everyone is a native English speaker. This is why we need to globalize such applications and make our content multilingual and culture-specific. This chapter will make the book more complete and rounded so that a developer can handle basic architecture and design issues while globalizing his or her ASP.NET web application.

In this chapter, we will learn:

- What globalization and localization is
- The best practices to follow while implementing globalization
- What resource files are
- How resource files are published
- Using the custom resource provider model for database based localization

In short, this chapter will explain all of the important concepts regarding globalization and localization both practically and comprehensively, and provide a practical step-by-step approach to globalizing a web application in ASP.NET 3.5 by following certain best practices.

Globalization and Localization

Globalization is defined as the process of developing a program or an application so that it is usable across multiple cultures and regions, irrespective of the language and regional differences. For example, say you have made a small inventory management program and you live in a region where English is the main language, such as the USA. Now, if you want to sell your program in a different country, say Germany, then you need to make sure that your program displays and accepts input in the German language as well, so that German users are able to use the same application.

Localization is the process of creating content, input, and output data, in a region-specific culture and language. Culture will determine date display format (such as, mm/dd/yyyy or dd/mm/yyyy), currency display format, and so on. The process by which we can make sure that our program will be localized is known as Internationalization or Globalization. In simpler terms, Globalization can be defined as the set of activities that will ensure that our program will be usable in regions with different languages and cultures. So globalization is the overall process whereby we change the code to support localized data, for example by using Resource files, and so on. Localization, on the other hand, is the process of using a particular culture and regional information so that the program uses the specific local languages and culture. This means translating text strings into a particular local language. This involves putting language-specific strings in the resource files. Globalization starts in the main construction phase, along with code development. Localization generally comes later.

Browser Settings

A user's browser has a default culture setting, which the browser uses to determine the most appropriate way to display content. In Internet Explorer, we can change the default language by going to **Internet Options** and clicking the **Language** button under **General** Tab:

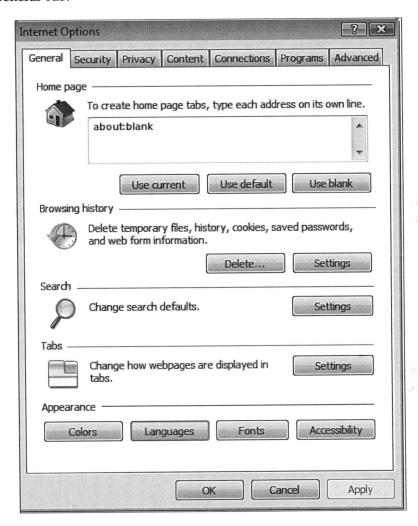

On the **General** tab, click the **Languages** button

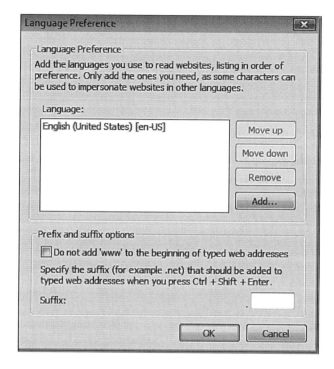

We can add new languages and change the default user language. Usually, this option is set to the computer's default culture where the browser was installed. As part of globalization, we have to make sure that our application is rendered correctly in different browsers on different computers having different default languages. So instead of letting the users change their browser language, our application should render the correct locale-specific content based on the users' language selection through our application.

Basic Steps for Globalizing an ASP.NET Website

Let's start with a simple example. For the purposes of explaining localization and keeping things simple, we will create a new website in ASP.NET and C# called **TestSite** (the source code of the example is included in this chapter). We will then add a master page and a default page. This default page has a `TextBox` and a `Calendar` control. The `TextBox` control has a `double` number which will represent currency, and we will see how the currency format varies as a user selects different languages.

Now, before we move ahead, let me throw some light on culture and locale.

Culture and Locale

Languages also depend upon the geographical location. For example, French is spoken in France as well as Canada (besides many other countries). But linguistically speaking, Canadian French is quite different from French spoken in France. Similarly, there are linguistic differences between US English and British English. Therefore, the language needs to be associated with the particular region where it is spoken, and this is done by using **Locale** (which is the combination of language and location).

For example, `fr` is the code for French language. `fr-FR` means French language in France. So, `fr` specifies only the language, whereas `fr-FR` is the locale. Similarly, `fr-CA` defines another locale implying French language and culture in Canada. If we use only `fr`, it implies a neutral culture (that is, location neutral).

How do we Define or Change the Current Culture?

There are two properties of the `CultureInfo` class in the .NET FCL (Framework Class Library) that we can set using the overloaded constructor of the class, and then use the class to change the culture of the currently executing thread:

- `UICulture`: This property gets or sets the user interface culture for the currently-executing thread. It helps the runtime to load the resource strings from a specific resource file (which we will see later). This property can take neutral cultures as well as locales. For example:

  ```
  Thread.CurrentThread.CurrentUICulture = new CultureInfo("fr");
  ```

  Or,

  ```
  Thread.CurrentThread.CurrentUICulture = new CultureInfo("fr-CA");
  ```

- `Culture`: This property gets or sets the region-specific culture and formats of currency, dates etc. This needs a language as well as location (locale). For example:

  ```
  //correct as we have given locale
  Thread.CurrentThread.CurrentCulture = new CultureInfo("fr-A");
  //wrong, will not work
  Thread.CurrentThread.CurrentCulture = new CultureInfo("fr");
  ```

Sometimes we need a culture that does not belong to any language or locale, and which is not a variant of any region/language. For this, we have the `CultureInfo.InvariantCulture` property. This is used during the internal system processes that need to be culture independent, or to store data that does not need to be displayed directly to the end user.

Both `UICulture` and `Culture` properties can be defined in the `Web.Config` file under the `<GLOBALIZATION>` property. They can also be specified at the page level. But we don't want to hard-code these values, and would like to set them dynamically instead. As seen above, we could also get or set these values from the code using the `Thread.CurrentThread.CurrentCulture` and `Thread.CurrentThread.CurrentUICulture` properties. So, we will use these properties in our application.

Switching Locale

Coming back to our application, we need a way to switch the locale. There are two approaches to this:

- **Use the browser settings:** In IE, the user can change the culture by going to **Internet Options | General | Languages**. For this to work, we need to set both the `Culture` and the `UICulture` to `auto` and `enableClientBasedCulture = true` as:

  ```
  <GLOBALIZATION culture="auto" uiculture="auto"
    enableClientBasedCulture=""true"" />
  ```

- **User specified settings:** We can provide an option for the user to specify and change the culture and the language at runtime. This is the recommended approach, as sometimes the browser itself may not have the user-specific culture set (for example, a French tourist might be surfing the net in India)., Further, changing language settings via the browser may also sometimes be blocked.

Following the second recommended approach, I have created a section on the top (inside a `Panel` control) in the master page where I have a drop-down with these language options, which lets the users choose a particular locale. For illustration purposes, I have only four language options to choose from: Hindi, US English, British English, and French.

For my application to be globalized, it is required that whenever the user selects a locale from the language, the following should happen:

- All content should be localized. This means that all strings and text should be displayed in the chosen language and locale.
- Each control's caption or content should also show the text in the local language.
- Date and currency formatting should be done according to the chosen locale.
- All messages displayed to the user should be in the local language.

To achieve these goals, the first thing you need to do is to take out content from the code and put it in separate resource files, which are simple XML files with a `.resx` extension in .NET.

Resource Files

Resource files are simple XML files that hold the localized unicode strings for different cultures and locale. Because this content will vary from language to language, we will have resource files for every culture. Resource files have a `.resx` extension and each `.resx` file has a key-value pair (name and value fields, just like a dictionary).

There are two types of resource files we can have in our application — **global resource** files and **local resource** files.

Global Versus Local Resources

Resource files can be saved in either the `App_GlobalResources` folder or the `App_LocalResources` folders in your project. The resource files under `App_LocalResources` are used for storing information that is not repeated across the pages (page-specific content), whereas `App_GlobalResorces` are used for storing site-wide content or content that is duplicated on multiple pages.

Before going ahead with the differences between global resources and local resources in detail, let us first see how we can create and add values in both global and local `.resx` files using Visual Studio (VS).

Creating Global Resources

Here is how we can add a simple value in three different global resource files (one for each culture) using VS. First of all, create a new web site in VS and name it **TestSite**. Then follow the steps below to create a simple demo page to test the localization (you can refer to the source code available on the website and use the sample project already created):

1. Add a Master Page to the project and name it `TestSiteMasterPage.master`.
2. Add a new ASPX page using that Master Page and name it `Default.aspx`.
3. Add two labels, a calendar control, and a textbox control on `Default.aspx`.
4. Add a new User Control named `Header.ascx`.
5. Add a drop-down in `Header.ascx` named `ddlLanguage`.
6. Add four hardcoded values in that drop-down. Here is the code:

```
<asp:DropDownList ID="ddlLanguage" runat="server"
                  AutoPostBack="True">
    <asp:ListItem Value="-1">Select a language</asp:ListItem>
    <asp:ListItem Value="0">Hindi</asp:ListItem>
    <asp:ListItem Value="1">US English</asp:ListItem>
    <asp:ListItem Value="2">GB English</asp:ListItem>
    <asp:ListItem Value="3">French</asp:ListItem>
</asp:DropDownList>
```

The following are the steps to create global resource files:

1. Right-click the website in VS, and select **Add New Item file**.

2. In the **Add New Item** dialog box, select **Resource File** and name it `TestSiteResources.resx` (you can actually use any name you like).

3. When you click the **Add** button, VS will ask you if you want to put this file under the `App_GlobalResources` folder. Select **Yes**.

4. Then, open the resource file in the VS editor (by double-clicking it).

5. Enter "Banner" in the **Name** field, and "Test Website for Localization" in the **Value** field. This resource file is the default for American English.

6. Add another resource file, and name it `TestSiteResources.fr-FR.resx`. This file is for French language strings.

7. Add "Banner" in the **Name** field, and "Examinez le site Web pour le comportement de localisation" in the **Value** field.

8. If you want to add Canadian French resources, then you need to create another resource file by the name of `TestSiteResources.fr-CA.resx`. The middle part of this name defines the locale, which should be the same as specified by the `UICulture` property.

In the same way, you can add more resource key values to the resource file for the controls we have on `Default.aspx` and `Header.ascx` in our website. Here is how the global resource files would look in VS **Solution Explorer**:

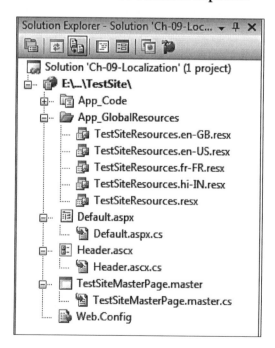

Creating Local Resources

Creating local resources is easy because we can use VS to generate local `.resx` files for our pages automatically. Here are the steps:

1   Select the `Default.aspx` file in the Solution Explorer.

2   Go to the **Tools** option in VS and select the **Generate Local Resource** option (this option will be visible only when you have selected an ASPX file in **Design Mode** or **Source Mode**; it will not be available when you are on a code-behind file). Here is how it should look:

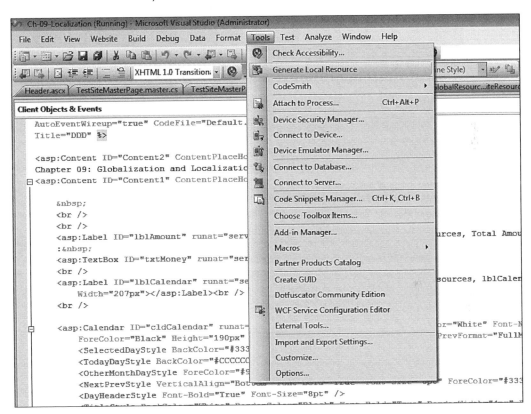

3   VS will automatically generate a `.resx` file under the `App_LocalResources` folder.

4   Edit that file and add values using VS.

5   Add more files in that folder for additional cultures as required.

If you want only certain pages to show the localized strings, you can restrict the localization behavior throughout the application by putting resource files in the `App_LocalDirectory` folder. This will make the localization page–specific, and not application-wide.

The naming of the `.resx` files should follow a certain pattern as shown here (assuming that you want to localize a page named `MyPage.aspx`):

- `MyPage.aspx.resx`: This is the default resource file for `MyPage.aspx`
- `MyPage.aspx.fr-FR.resx`: This will be used when the culture changes to French, though only `MyPage.aspx` in the application would be localized

Choosing between Global and Local Resources

Global resource files should be used when we have content that is common across multiple pages in our website. For example, text such as the company name and address can be repeated on many pages, so these items should be put in global resources files. But if we put all of our content only in global resource files, then we will be overloading `App_GlobalResources` and it can grow in size, making it difficult to manage and update the `.resx` file. For large applications having a lot of content in a single resource file, there can be a performance impact.

On the other hand, if we put all of the data only in the local resource files, then there would be a resource file for every page, which would create a lot of maintenance issues. Also, resources inside local resource files cannot be shared with other pages or controls in our website, which means that we would have to duplicate common content in multiple local resource files. So we need to strike a balance by putting only page-specific content in the local resource files and putting generic content in the global resource files.

Satellite Assemblies

All of the resource files are compiled into assemblies at runtime. These assemblies are known as "satellite assemblies", and have strongly-typed wrappers for the XML resource files. So we don't need to worry about creating resource assemblies in ASP. NET. These assemblies are placed in separate folders (according to the name of the locale) under the `/bin` folder, after you have published your website:

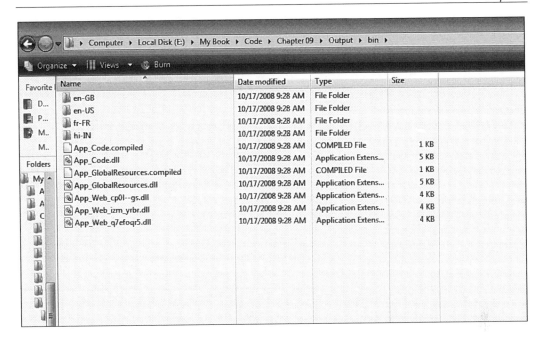

Now that we have created the resource files for the different cultures and languages, we need a way to load them at runtime when the user dynamically changes their culture. Fortunately, implementing this in ASP.NET 3.5 is quite easy. See the following code:

```
String welcome = Resources.TestSiteResources.Welcome;
```

In this line of code, we are using the `Resources` namespace, which was created automatically by ASP.NET when it compiled the resource files into satellite assemblies. We use the `TestSiteResources` class, with the same name as that of the resource file we created. We then access the `Welcome` property, which will give the actual text from the resource file, based on the current culture.

Implicit Versus Explicit Localization

If we want to localize the text of the `Label` control `lblWelcome`, we can do the same thing using these methods, in ASP.NET 3.5:

- **Implicit localization:** Here, we specify the new `meta` tags in the control definition and let ASP.NET get the value from the resource files based on the `resourcekey` attribute:

```
<asp:Label id=lblWelcome meta:resourcekey="lblWelcome"
                Text="Welcome" runat="server">

</asp:Label>
```

For this to work, we need to have page-specific resource files in the /App_LocalDirectory folder. Implicit localization helps in trimming down the size of the global resource files which further helps in overall resource management. We should use implicit localization when we have mostly page-specific content.

We do not need to do anything manually to set these implicit localization properties. Just open your web page in the Design mode, go to **Tools | Generate Local Resources**. This will automatically create a resource file for your page. You only need to set the values (Control.Property) of different fields for each control in the resource file editor in VS.

- **Explicit localization:** This works when we have global resource files. Here, we use expressions to set the values from the resource files, as shown below:

```
<asp:Label id=lblWelcome Text="<%$Resources:TestSiteResources,
                        Welcome %>"
        runat="server"></asp:Label>
```

We can set this using the VS IDE. Select the **Label** control, go to the **Properties** window, and select **Expressions | Text**. Then, choose **Resources** from the drop-down list and enter the class name (TestSiteResources, for this example) and the **Resource key** (Banner). This is the recommended way to localize the UI controls on a page.

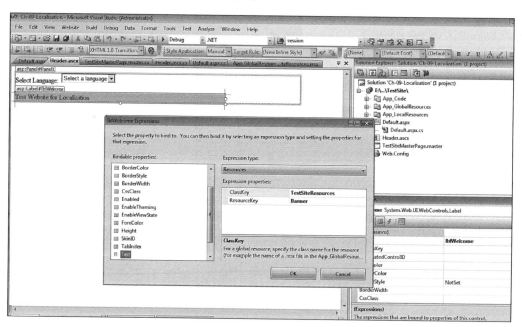

- **Programmatically accessing strongly-typed resource classes**: This can be achieved by using the following code:

```
lblWelcome.Text = Resources.TestSiteResources.Welcome;
```

This will work, but it needs to be coded for every control on the page. Therefore, it is better to use the second method (Explicit localization) for all of the controls, and use this method to access resource strings for other content, if needed. Also, note that controls such as the `Calendar` control have in-built localization. As soon as the `UICulture` and `Culture` of the current thread changes, it shows localized content by itself, thanks to ASP.NET!

Incorporating Globalization

In our sample website, after creating the resource files and creating some localized data, we first start using the explicit localization to set the text of the controls such as the `Labels` in our web site so that they get their values from the resource files. Because in our example there are four languages, let us create four resource files, along with a fifth fallback resource file (with no locale name). Here is a screenshot of these files:

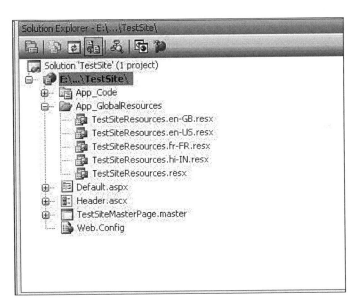

Note that the resource files have the locale as their middle names, so we need to set the `UICulture` to the same named locale so that ASP.NET can access these resource files.

But the problem is, how do we change the culture dynamically on the postback event? Fortunately, ASP.NET provides a method in the `Page` class to override `InitializeCulture()`. This method executes very early in the page life cycle (much before any control is generated), and here we can set the `UICulture` and `Culture` of the current thread.

Because this method is in the `Page` class and we do not want to repeat the same code for each web page, let us create a `BasePage` class, and all of the ASPX pages in our application will be derived from this `BasePage` class. Before moving ahead with the code for this method, let us understand how we can set the culture and maintain its state throughout postbacks.

Setting the Culture of the Thread Based on User Selection

Going back to the UI design we created earlier, we had a `MasterPage` and a `Header` user control in it (inside a `ContentPlaceHolder`). We had a default page associated with that `MasterPage`. The entire site had to be localized dynamically. So in the header control, there was a drop-down from where the user could select a language and culture. In the `BasePage`'s `InitilializeCulture` method, we have to get the value of the item the user has selected from the drop-down. But, we have a problem here.

The `InitializeCulture()` method is fired very early in the page life cycle. At that stage, none of the controls on the page have been initialized. So we cannot access any control directly like this:

```
String userLanguage = ddlLanguage.SelectedValue;
```

The only way to access the user selection from the drop-down control is to use the `Form` collection (from the `Response` object). Here is the code to do this:

```
public const string LanguageDropDownID =
        "ctl00$cphHeader$Header1$ddlLanguage";
public const string PostBackEventTarget = "__EVENTTARGET";
```

Here, we are using the `"parentControl$ChildControl"` syntax to access the control from the `Form` collection. You can access any nested control generated by ASP. NET by using this convention. Using this value of the selected item from the `Form` collection, we can set the culture in a `switch case` statement, as follows:

```
protected override void InitializeCulture()
{
    if(Request[PostBackEventTarget] != null)
    {
        string controlID = Request[PostBackEventTarget];
```

```
        if(controlID.Equals(LanguageDropDownID))
        {
        string selectedValue =
        Request.Form[Request[PostBackEventTarget]].ToString();
    switch (selectedValue)
        {
    case "0": SetCulture("hi-IN", "hi-IN");
    break;
    case "1": SetCulture("en-US", "en-US");
    break;
    case "2": SetCulture("en-GB", "en-GB");
    break;
    case "3": SetCulture("fr-FR", "fr-FR");
    break;
    default: break;
        }
        }
    }
    if (Session["MyUICulture"] != null &&
        Session["MyCulture"] != null)
    {
    Thread.CurrentThread.CurrentUICulture
    = (CultureInfo)Session["MyUICulture"];
    Thread.CurrentThread.CurrentCulture
    = (CultureInfo)Session["MyCulture"];
    }
    base.InitializeCulture();
}
protected void SetCulture(string name, string locale)
{
    Thread.CurrentThread.CurrentUICulture
    = new CultureInfo(name);
    Thread.CurrentThread.CurrentCulture
    = new CultureInfo(locale);
    Session["MyUICulture"]
    = Thread.CurrentThread.CurrentUICulture;
    Session["MyCulture"] = Thread.CurrentThread.CurrentCulture;
}
```

We first check if the postback has happened due to the language drop-down's selection changed event. We do not want to change the culture on every postback, but only when the user selects a language from the language drop-down. Again, here is the code:

```
if(Request[PostBackEventTarget] != null)
    {
            string controlID = Request[PostBackEventTarget];
            if (controlID.Equals(LanguageDropDownID))
```

Next, we get the value of the item the user selected from the language selection drop-down:

```
string selectedValue =
Request.Form[Request[PostBackEventTarget]].ToString();
```

Then, we use a switch case statement and call the SetCulture() method based on the different locale values, as follows:

```
switch (selectedValue)
        {
        case "0": SetCulture("hi-IN", "hi-IN");
        break;
        case "1": SetCulture("en-US", "en-US");
        break;
        case "2": SetCulture("en-GB", "en-GB");
        break;
        case "3": SetCulture("fr-FR", "fr-FR");
        break;
        default: break;
        }
        }
    }
```

In the Setculture() method, we simply set the current thread's Culture and UICulture properties to the user's selected locale-specific culture:

```
protected void SetCulture(string name, string locale)
    {
        Thread.CurrentThread.CurrentUICulture
        = new CultureInfo(name);
        Thread.CurrentThread.CurrentCulture
        = new CultureInfo(locale);
        Session["MyUICulture"]
        = Thread.CurrentThread.CurrentUICulture;
        Session["MyCulture"] = Thread.CurrentThread.CurrentCulture;
    }
```

We need to save the `Culture` selected in a session or a cookie variable because if the user moves to some other page in the same application, the thread's culture information would be lost as the new `Page` class will instantiate from the beginning (HTTP is stateless!). Cookies can be used if you do not want to lose the current thread's `Culture` on the user's session expiry.

Once we have pulled out all localizable static content from the web application and moved it into the resource files, and set the `Culture` and `UICulture` based on the user's choice, we are ready with our globalization framework. Now, the only thing left is the addition of resource-specific data in the resource files. For each culture, we need to have a separate (and appropriately named) resource file. This process is localization.

In the `web.config` file, we have used the following properties:

```
<globalization responseEncoding"=utf-8" requestEncoding="utf-8"
                fileEncoding="utf-8" />
```

Note the encoding attributes—`UTF-8` (8-bit Unicode Transformation Format) is used as it is variable-length character encoding and can represent languages such as Greek, Arabic, and so on, in addition to being ASCII compatible. For more information on `UTF-8` encoding, refer to link: `http://en.wikipedia.org/wiki/UTF-8`.

Also, an important point to be noted here is that although we can have the resource files in raw XML format on the deployment server (so that the user can edit them without re-compiling the entire site), the application will re-start if we make any modification to the resource files. This can hamper the performance of the deployed application.

dir Attribute for Language Direction

Sometimes we may also need to set the direction of the localized text (which is set using the `dir` attribute of the `<html>` or the `<body>` tag). This is necessary because some languages are read from **right-to-left** (**RTL**) as is the case in Arabic for example, instead of the standard **left-to-right** (**LTR**) style used in Hindi and English. This can be achieved quite easily by setting the `dir` attribute to the appropriate value from the `.resx` file.

First, create a "direction" (you can use any name) field in all your resource files, setting its property to RTL or LTR based on the individual resource files. For Arabic, the value of this field would be RTL, and for Hindi it would be LTR. Then, set the same in the `dir` attribute of the `<body>` tag as:

```
<body runat="server" dir="<%$ Resources: TestSiteResources, Direction
%>">
```

This will set the correct text direction, as the value will come from the resource file based on the current thread's culture.

Editing Resource Files after publishing in ASP.NET 3.5

An important point to note when globalizing your ASP.NET 3.5 web applications is the dynamic updating of the .resx files once published on the remote server. We would like to have this flexibility so that the users can modify the values in the XML resource files (.resx files) themselves once the application is deployed on a server, without using VS and republishing the files. The ability to do this depends on the project model we have followed for our web application in VS.

If we are using the **WebSite Project model** (which is the default in VS), then only the resource files under the App_LocalResources will get published as raw .resx files on the server, as they are not compiled. These resource files can be edited on the server (as they are compiled during runtime). Files under the App_GlobalResources folder are compiled into individual resource-specific DLLs and published on the server. So you cannot edit the resource files that are under App_GlobalResources once they have been published using the WebSite project model, as it has a default pre-compiled web deployment model. If you need to add new locale resources, then you can either do so in VS, and recompile and republish the application, or you can first manually generate the new resource file using the tool resgen.exe and then compile it to a satellite assembly using the **Assembly Linker tool.**

If we are using a **Web Application Project (WAP)** model, then the files under both the App_GlobalResources and App_LocalResources folders will get published as raw .resx files that are editable. So using WAP gives you this slight flexibility, which the default WebSite model does not provide.

Whenever we change any resource file (local or global) under the / bin folder of the deployed web application, an application restart will occur, which may cause the loss of data (such as values stored in session variables, and so on). This happens because ASP.NET caches the resource file contents in memory, and if the content has changed, the in-memory cache needs to be re-loaded from the updated content.

Entering Foreign Language Characters: Input Method Editor (IME)

Sometimes, we need to enter different language characters in the input controls of our web site to test localization. Say we have made a localizable web site and would like to test this by entering, for example, French characters. This can be done easily by using the **Input Method Editor** (IME) in Windows, which is a convenient tool to change the keyboard layout to support another language set allowing the entry of complex characters for languages such as Chinese, Japanese, and so on.

To start the IME:

1. Go to the **Control Panel** and open **Regional and Language Options**.

2. Go to the **Keyboards and Languages** tab and click the **Change keyboards...** button. See the following screenshot:

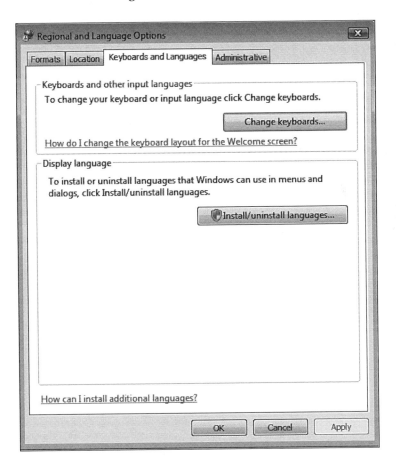

3. You will see the **Text Services and Input Languages** dialog box, as shown in the following screenshot:

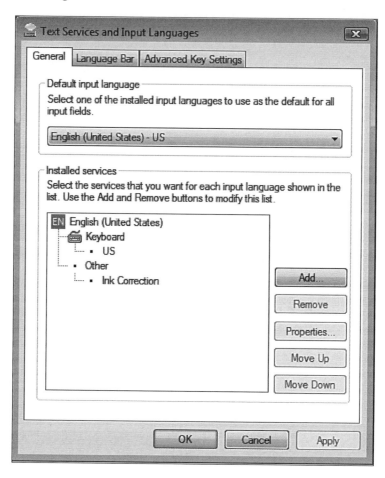

4. In the screenshot, the default language is English. To add additional languages, click the **Add** button and select the language you need (see the following screenshot):

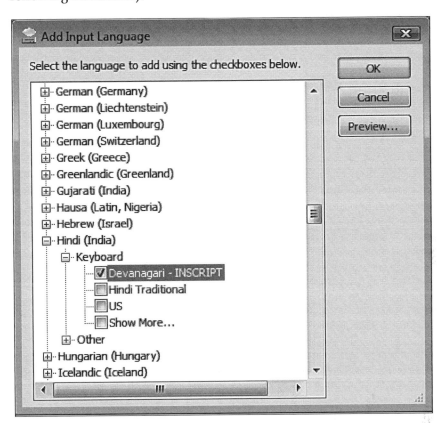

5. This particular example will add the Hindi Language keyboard. Click the **OK** button to save your changes, and exit the **Control Panel**. You will see the language bar on the top right of your desktop, and you can click the language button and switch languages accordingly. You can use a Hindi keyboard to enter Hindi Unicode characters in the resource files.

In this way, you can switch to different languages and enter characters in your test web site to check the localization. There is an excellent article on how to use IME to enter Japanese, Korean, and Chinese language characters, available via the following link:

```
http://www.microsoft.com/globaldev/handson/user/IME_Paper.mspx
```

Using a Database for Localization

We have seen how to localize the text of the controls and the application content in the UI. But sometimes, the content is stored in a database, and this content also needs to be localized (for example, when using a Content Management System). Because this content is stored in a database, we cannot use resource files for this. Sometimes we may not be able to use resource files at all because we might want to avoid an application recompilation or restart when updating localized content (remember that updating a resource file under the /bin folder will cause an application recompilation or an application restart.).

Also, using a database gives us the flexibility to edit content easily as there are no resource files involved. We can create a simple edit form, so that content authors can edit and update the content without having any programming knowledge.

Custom Resource-Provider-Model in ASP.NET

When we use a database instead of .resx files to store the localized content in our application, we will need to make sure that we can access the resources using implicit as well as explicit localization, and get different localized content based on changing the current thread's locale. In short, we will need to create a similar framework to the one that ASP.NET provided us with when using .resx files.

Fortunately, in ASP.NET 3.5, this process is made easy by extending the **Resource-Provider-Model** and creating a custom database-based resource provider. Using the provider model will help us to leverage the ASP.NET infrastructure to manage localized resources from a database and use its API for performing the same tasks as for the XML based .resx files. Because the Resource-Provider-Model has a simple implementation approach, we will not study it in detail in this chapter. You can refer to the links given here for a detailed step-by-step example of how to extend the Resource-Provider-model to use a database instead of the .resx files:

```
http://www.west-wind.com/presentations/wwDbResourceProvider/
```

Summary

In this chapter, we have covered some important aspects of implementing globalization in ASP.NET 3.5. We saw that although it is easy and simple, there are a few important points and best practices to bear in mind when globalizing our ASP. NET web applications:

- Do not rely on the web browser's settings. Provide a link on the application (may be in the header) so that the users can select their choice of language.

- Use .resx files to separate out presentation-related data in the GUI. Resource fallback is the approach used by ASP.NET when it is unable to find the resource file for a particular culture. It will first go to the neutral resource file, and then to the default or fallback resource file.

- Strike a balance between global and local resource files based on the application's needs.

- We can extend the Resource-Provider-Model in ASP.NET to store localized content in database tables instead of the .resx files. This gives us the flexibility to modify and update localized content easily at runtime without disturbing the main application.

In the nine chapters of this book so far, we saw and understood how to architect and design our ASP.NET web applications based on our actual project needs. We also learnt about the various architectural options, and when to use a particular approach over the other considering the scope, complexity and long term goals of our projects.

To summarize, a good architecture should take into consideration the following list of parameters:

- scalability
- reusability
- interpretability
- flexibility
- maintainability
- security
- robustness
- readability

Each of the above parameter plays a decisive role in forming the core architecture of our projects. In this book, we have studied only a few approaches but there can be potentially infinite ways to program and develop applications, and it's impossible to learn and study them all. There are many ways in which we can structure and develop our applications, and no particular architecture or design is a perfect solution. Moreover, an architecture designed for a particular scenario might not work well in other cases. So the best strategy is to understand the current as well as the future business needs of the project and decide on which architecture will best suit the long-term and as well as short-term goals.

Index

C

W

WCF
  about 180
  components 181
  sample project 181, 182, 183
web application
  big applications 160, 161
  categories 160
  default N-tier nature 32, 33
  sample configuration 32
  small application 160, 161

Web Service Enhancements. *See* **WSE**
Windows Communication Foundation.
    See **WCF**
WSE 180

X

XML web services
  about 167, 168
XML
  selecting, tips 188, 189

Thank you for buying
ASP.NET 3.5

About Packt Publishing

Packt, pronounced 'packed', published its first book "*Mastering phpMyAdmin for Effective MySQL Management*" in April 2004 and subsequently continued to specialize in publishing highly focused books on specific technologies and solutions.

Our books and publications share the experiences of your fellow IT professionals in adapting and customizing today's systems, applications, and frameworks. Our solution based books give you the knowledge and power to customize the software and technologies you're using to get the job done. Packt books are more specific and less general than the IT books you have seen in the past. Our unique business model allows us to bring you more focused information, giving you more of what you need to know, and less of what you don't.

Packt is a modern, yet unique publishing company, which focuses on producing quality, cutting-edge books for communities of developers, administrators, and newbies alike. For more information, please visit our website: www.packtpub.com.

Writing for Packt

We welcome all inquiries from people who are interested in authoring. Book proposals should be sent to author@packtpub.com. If your book idea is still at an early stage and you would like to discuss it first before writing a formal book proposal, contact us; one of our commissioning editors will get in touch with you.

We're not just looking for published authors; if you have strong technical skills but no writing experience, our experienced editors can help you develop a writing career, or simply get some additional reward for your expertise.

ASP.NET Data Presentation Controls Essentials

ISBN: 978-1-847193-95-7   Paperback: 250 pages

Master the standard ASP.NET server controls for displaying and managing data

1. Systematic coverage of major ASP.NET data presentation controls

2. Packed with re-usable examples of common data control tasks

3. Covers LINQ and binding data to ASP.NET 3.5 (Orcas) controls

Entity Framework Tutorial

ISBN: 978-1-847195-22-7   Paperback: 250 pages

Learn to build a better data access layer with the ADO.NET Entity Framework and ADO.NET Data Services

1. Clear and concise guide to the ADO.NET Entity Framework with plentiful code examples

2. Create Entity Data Models from your database and use them in your applications

3. Learn about the Entity Client data provider and create statements in Entity SQL

4. Learn about ADO.NET Data Services and how they work with the Entity Framework

Please check **www.PacktPub.com** for information on our titles

ASP.NET 3.5 Social Networking

An expert guide to building enterprise ready social networking and community applications with ASP.NET 3.5

Andrew Siemer

ASP.NET 3.5 Social Networking

ISBN: 978-1-847194-78-7   Paperback: 613 pages

An expert guide to building enterprise-ready social networking and community applications with ASP.NET 3.5

1. Create a full-featured, enterprise-grade social network using ASP.NET 3.5

2. Learn key new ASP.NET topics in a practical, hands-on way: LINQ, AJAX, C# 3.0, n-tier architectures, and MVC

3. Build friends lists, messaging systems, user profiles, blogs, message boards, groups, and more

4. Rich with example code, clear explanations, interesting examples, and practical advice – a truly hands-on book for ASP.NET developers

Building Websites with the ASP.NET Community Starter Kit

A practical guide to understanding, implementing, and extending the powerful and free application from Microsoft

K. Scott Allen
Cristian Darie

Building Websites with the ASP.NET Community Starter Kit

ISBN: 1-904811-00-0   Paperback: 268 pages

A comprehensive guide to understanding, implementing, and extending the powerful and freely available application from Microsoft

1. Learn .NET architecture through building real-world examples

2. Understand, implement, and extend the Community Starter Kit

3. Learn to create and customize your own website

4. For ASP.NET developers with a sound grasp of C#

Please check **www.PacktPub.com** for information on our titles

13467024R00149

Made in the USA
Lexington, KY
01 February 2012